The Copyright Book

William S. Strong

**The Copyright Book:
A Practical Guide**

Third edition

The MIT Press
Cambridge, Massachusetts
London, England

Second Printing, 1990

©1981, 1984, 1990
Massachusetts Institute of
Technology

This book was set in Palatino by
Graphic Composition, Athens, GA
and printed and bound by
Halliday Lithograph in the United
States of America.

**Library of Congress Cataloging-in-
Publication Data**

Strong, William S.
     The copyright book: a practical guide /
William S. Strong.—3rd ed.
          p.   cm.
     Bibliography: p.
     Includes index.
     ISBN 0-262-19292-6
     1. Copyright—United States.   I. Title.
KF2994.S75   1990
346.7304'82—dc20
[347.306482]   89-34737
                                          CIP

For my parents

Contents

Preface to the Third Edition

As has often been observed, we notice change less when we live with it day by day. Thus I had not fully perceived how dramatically copyright has changed over the past five years until I sat down to the task of bringing this book up to date.

During those five years Congress has amended the law four times: to accomplish U.S. adherence to the Berne Convention, to protect the masks used in making semiconductor chips, to give music owners control over phonorecord rentals, and to give compulsory licenses to certain owners of satellite dish receivers. The Supreme Court has radically altered what was conventional wisdom regarding ownership of commissioned works. And the cumulative evolution of case law has continued, like the sea, to erode here and build up there, especially where computer software is concerned.

Why all this activity? Part of the cause is the law's never-ending attempt to catch up with technological evolution. Part is the determination of certain key players in Washington, D.C. to wrap up unfinished business; U.S. adherence to Berne was unattainable in the 1976 revision, but those who were committed to it bided their time and finally succeeded in 1988. And part is the sheer volume of copyright litigation;

the more cases are decided, the more doctrine is likely to be affected.

There is no end in sight to this rapid change. As copyright becomes more and more important in our economy, Congress and the courts will be asked to make more and more hard decisions. For there is no denying that many decisions remain to be made.

With full knowledge of its limited life expectancy, then, I offer you this revised and updated study of the law of copyright. I am deeply grateful to the many readers who have made this little book a standard reference of sorts, and I will try to retain their good will by staying abreast of change.

I am grateful in another vein to Michelle Sabbag, who has typed and retyped so well without complaint most of the revisions of this book, and to my editor, Larry Cohen, a master at balancing the goad and the sympathetic ear.

Preface

At their best, our laws embody our deepest assumptions about human beings and what proper relations among human beings ought to be. Copyright is such a law. It springs from the belief that those who try to contribute to our always inadequate store of information and inspiration ought to be paid for their pains. This seems a very creditable attitude.

My purpose in writing this book has been to make available to people whose lives and work are affected by the laws of copyright an understanding of their rights and responsibilities. However, I hope that in doing so I have also managed to communicate some of my own fascination with the subject.

A new copyright law came into effect on January 1, 1978, overturning much that had gone before. It has enormous implications for authors and artists, not only in traditional media but in computer programming and other new areas of communication technology as well. It has equally great impact on those who use copyrighted works: teachers, performers, librarians, business people. So from both points of view, the time seems ripe for this project.

I have found it useful to write much of this book as though from the standpoint of the creator of a work—be it a novel, a painting, a blueprint, a dance.

But whatever is not kept safe for the artist is given to the public; if you are a would-be user of an artistic or other creative work, you will know your boundaries by the boundaries drawn for the creator of it.

I have tried to gather material and organize it in a way that will tell the story simply. This has not proved possible in all respects; parts of the law are so complex that no amount of pruning and rearranging could make them any less dense. Nor has it proved possible at every point to avoid technical language and terms whose legal definition differs from their ordinary meaning. In such places I have given examples to try to make clear what is being said.

Two further comments about organization are in order. First, because the new copyright law governs all works created after 1977 and many aspects of works created earlier, I have used the new law as my guide for most of this book. If you are concerned with pre-1978 works, you should be sure to read chapter 9, which deals with these works. Second, although many rules differ from one art form to another, it became apparent that to deal with various art forms individually would create a great deal of needless repetition. Instead, therefore, I have treated the various aspects of the law as units and within each unit discussed the exceptions pertaining to one art form or another. It may be helpful to see the exceptions set out in this manner.

Space does not permit me to acknowledge adequately the encouragement of family and friends in the writing of this book. However, I do want to take the occasion to thank the staff at my former firm, Herrick & Smith, without whom all encouragement would have been in vain. In particular I thank Evie Hanlon and the Word Processing Crew, whose skill and patience were beyond measure.

The Copyright Book

1 The Subject Matter of Copyright

Copyright law is essentially a system of property. Like property in land, you can sell it, leave it to your heirs, donate it, or lease it under any sort of conditions; you can divide it into separate parts; you can protect it from almost every kind of trespass. Also, like property in land, copyrights can be subjected to certain kinds of public use that are considered to be in the public interest. I shall explain these various aspects of copyright property through the course of this book.

The province of copyright is communication. It does not deal with machines or processes—those are governed by patent law—or with titles, slogans, and the other symbols that businesses use to distinguish themselves in the public eye, for that is the stuff of trademark law. Works of art and literature are what copyright protects, no matter what the medium, and works whose purpose is to convey information or ideas. In the words of the statute, it protects "original works of authorship fixed in any tangible medium of expression, now known or later developed, from which they can be perceived, reproduced, or otherwise communicated, either directly or with the aid of a machine or device."[1]

This seemingly simple bit of language incorporates

three of the fundamental concepts of the law, concepts whose meaning must be clearly grasped before all else: fixation, originality, and expression.

Fixation

Fixation is the act of rendering a creation in some tangible form in which, or by means of which, other people can perceive it. Even the word *perceive* has its special legal meaning; in the law's definition one "perceives" a work of choreography, for example, or a work of music, by seeing on a piece of paper the notation that enables a performer to reproduce the work. Thus a musical work may be fixed in sheet music, as well as on tape. On the other hand performing the musical work, without taping it simultaneously, does not fix it because the performance is not tangible. It is heard and is gone.

The great importance of the act of fixation is that it marks the beginning of your federal copyright. You obtain copyright under the federal law as of the instant that you fix your work in tangible form. Fixation also draws the boundary line between federal copyright protection and so-called common law copyright, which is largely the prerogative of the individual states. (*Common law* is the term for law that is built up over the years by judicial opinions; in the copyright field there has not been a great deal of variation from one state to another.)

Until January 1, 1978, common law copyright protected all unpublished works except those that were registered with the U.S. Copyright Office; now it protects only works that have not been fixed in tangible form.[2] If, for example, you have developed a pantomime in your head, but have not written any notes about it that would enable another performer to reproduce it, your unfixed work falls under the protection of common law copyright. You may perform it as often as you like, or you can let others perform it for a fee, and no one else may copy it. Presumably also you can bequeath the right to perform it to your children, and they to their children. After your death, though, it will grow increasingly more difficult to prove just what your common law copyright consisted of and who owns it.

Not much more of substance can be said at this point about common law copyright. Rights in works that have not been fixed are difficult to prove and difficult to protect; it is not even easy to prove what the work is if there is no tangible copy of it. Because the new federal law has so severely restricted the operation of the common law, this book is devoted to works that are fixed and thus governed by the federal law, except where I specifically state otherwise.

Originality

The law requires that a work be the product of your own mind in order to be copyrightable. Originality is not by itself sufficient; facts, even if they are facts that no one else has ever discovered, are regarded as the common property of all of us, as are scientific discoveries, mathematical equations, and historical theories.[3] Facts are not copyrightable because they are not human inventions; theories are not copyrightable because they are ideas, not expression. But although originality is not sufficient in itself, it is essential all the same.

The law follows a highly subjective theory of originality that often surprises, and sometimes shocks, those encountering it for the first time. If asked whether a person can get a copyright for something that has been created by someone else, most people would answer "no," but that answer would not always be correct. It is true that you cannot get a valid copyright in material that you have taken from someone else's work. But if you have recreated a pre-existing work without having had access to it or knowledge of it, you can enforce your copyright against anyone who has actually copied from you, regardless of the fact that that person might have copied with equal ease from the preexisting work. This conundrum is a great favorite of copyright scholars. "If by some magic," one has argued, "a man who had never known it were to compose anew Keat's Ode on a Grecian Urn, he would be an 'author,' and . . . others might not copy that poem, though they might of course copy Keat's."[4] It is said to illustrate the difference between copyright and patent (which is based on objective originality), and indeed it does. Whether at its extremes that difference should be a source of pride is less clear.

That elements of your work may be in the public domain does not invalidate your entire copyright. It only limits your copyright to what is original with you.

An original exposition of public domain material may take the form of arrangement. For example, *The Waste Land* is clearly a copyrightable poem, even though many of its lines are taken from works that are in the public domain. Eliot's originality lies in the juxtaposition of these public domain elements, and his copyright extends only to the limits of his originality. Similarly, a collage of newspaper clippings is a copyrightable arrangement.

Of a slightly different nature, but copyrightable on the same basic principle, are works the law calls "derivative works." Derivative works are those in which someone else's creation is "recast, transformed, or adapted."[5] Translations, sound recordings that transform musical or other works into magnetic notation, movie versions of plays or stories, orchestrations of melodies, and dolls based on cartoon characters are all obvious examples of derivative works. Others are less obvious but equally common, such as art reproductions. A mezzotint reproduction of a painting might seem to be a copy rather than a derivative work entitled to a protection in its own right, but in fact it is regarded as a derivative work. The reasoning behind this is that the manufacture of an art reproduction in a medium different from that of the original requires the reproducer to contribute some measure of his own special skill, and that contribution is entitled to protection. In fact it has even been held that an exact reproduction of a piece of sculpture, substantially reduced in scale, can be copyrighted as a derivative work if the making of it requires great artistic skill and effort.[6]

A derivative work may be made of a copyrighted work or of a work in the public domain. If it is of a copyrighted work, and if the artist has not authorized it, the work will constitute an infringement of the artist's copyright. In any event the protection afforded to a derivative work extends only to the original contribution of the maker.[7]

Would Eliot's *The Waste Land* be regarded as a derivative work? Would *West Side Story* be regarded as a derivative work of *Romeo and Juliet?* Would Moussorgsky's *Pictures at an Exhibition* be regarded as a derivative work of the pictures that inspired him? The answer to all three of these questions is "no." It may be helpful to analyze why.

Partly the question is one of motive. Eliot's use of preexisting poems was intended not to recast those works in another medium but to use them, through parody and juxtaposition, as building blocks for a message uniquely his own. It was not Eliot's intent, nor was it his achievement, merely to create a new version of Marvell's *To His Coy Mistress* when he wrote

But at my back from time to time I hear
The sound of horns and motors which shall bring
Sweeney to Mrs. Porter in the spring.

Similarly, *West Side Story* is not based on *Romeo and Juliet* in the way that the movie *Gone with the Wind* was based on Margaret Mitchell's novel; it attempts not to tell Shakespeare's story in another medium but to tell its own story, which resembles Shakespeare's play in many important respects. (If *Romeo and Juliet* were still under copyright, *West Side Story* would be an infringement, but that is another matter.)

Partly too the question is one of recognizability. Quite simply one does not recognize particular pictures in Moussorgsky's composition. Recognizability is not perhaps a firm and reassuring principle, but it is nonetheless an important one in determining derivativeness.

Another category of derivative works that deserves mention is that described in the statute as works "consisting of editorial revisions, annotations, elaborations, or other modifications which, as a whole, represent an original work of authorship." What the law protects here is the original contribution of the editor or annotator. The law will not protect trivial modifications, but it will protect modifications that are sweeping enough to constitute a "new version" of the preexisting work. The protection given a revision would cover only the work of the editor's own creativity. If a scholar, on the basis of research, revises the text of, say, a poem by Spenser, he cannot get a copyright in the new text because what he has done is to restore Spenser's own words.

The amount of originality required for a derivative work to be eligible for copyright is not as clear-cut as the earlier mention of mezzotints and reduced-scale sculptures might suggest. Recent cases have shown a tightening of the rules, with results that may in the end prove unfortunate. The same court (the Second Circuit Court of Appeals) that in 1951 upheld the copyright of mezzotints struck down, in 1976, the copyright of an Uncle Sam mechanical bank that was a smaller-scale version of earlier, public domain models but with certain features altered. In 1980 it denied copyright to three-dimensional models of cartoon characters. And in 1983 another federal court (the Seventh Circuit) denied copyright to paintings that were based on movie stills. At present only one Court of Appeals still holds to the more liberal standard of earlier cases; when last heard from on this subject, in 1962, the Ninth Circuit was willing to grant copyright to a three-dimensional plastic Santa Claus and protect it at least against slavish copying.[8] In 1951 all that was required for copyright was that the author have contributed a "distinguishable variation"; now, for some courts at least, the variation must also be "substantial." This new substantiality requirement is out of sync with the general standard of originality that applies elsewhere in the law.

Those judges who have taken the more restrictive view seem particularly worried that a looser standard will make it difficult in litigation to determine which work was being copied, the original or the derivative. Also they seem to fear the creation of traps by those who slyly place copyright notices on works to which they have made covert alterations. These fears seem exaggerated. If we apply the "distinguishable variation" test, it will be easy to know whether a defendant has copied the original or the derivative work by whether the variation appears in the defendant's product. As for traps, two things can be said. First, if the variation is truly distinguishable, forcing the would-be copyist to go to the original source does not seem all that oppressive.[9] Second, those who set such traps can always (and usually should) be punished by the courts when the traps are sprung in litigation, by granting attorneys' fees to the defendants.

The substantiality doctrine will, if taken too far, make it impossible for one who adapts a work to a new medium to get a copyright without making changes in the content of the work as well. Certainly, as things stand now, an adaptation of a work to another medium, or to a larger or smaller scale, will be likely to obtain copyright only if it either requires great artistic skill and labor to make or substantially varies from the original.

Authors should always bear in mind that the right to create derivative works is part of copyright. Thus, if an author transfers all rights in a work to someone else, this right goes with the rest. The author would no longer be able, for example, to create new versions of his work. This is often an important negotiating point in copyright agreements.

The law's protection of art reproductions as derivative works illustrates, perhaps in an extreme way, its regard for originality, wherever found. But the law also protects, within the category known as "compilations" (which comprises everything from *The Oxford Book of English Verse* to the *Yellow Pages*), a vast number of works that have no originality whatever: airline guides, telephone directories, catalogs, and so on. Some courts will require that the compiler have used some subjective judgment in selecting and arranging the information. Others protect "industrious collection" as authorship in and for itself.[10] But what is really being protected in all such cases is the economic value of the work put into them. The scope of the copyright is understandably narrow. If you put out, say, a catalog of the works of a painter, which contains lists almost identical to someone else's, you are not necessarily infringing copyright in the earlier catalog. You will be held liable only if you have taken a free ride on the first writer's labor; if as a result of your own investigations you arrive at the same results, you will be able to get your own copyright.[11] Where you are using the first writer's work as a data base for making a compilation that might be called a "derivative work" of the earlier work, the courts will generally require that you at least go to the trouble of independently verifying the data you use.[12]

When a derivative work gets its own copyright, this copyright is limited, like all other copyrights, to whatever material is original with the creator. An English translation of *Anna Karenina* is a derivative work, and it can be copyrighted, but the copyright will be narrowly defined to avoid giving the translator any kind of rights in what was actually created by Tolstoy. The translator will be protected against someone who copies his translation but not against someone who makes a similar translation by independent effort. Another example would be the musical version of *Oliver Twist*. Without doubt the musical *Oliver* is copyrightable, but only to the extent that its characters, its plot, and its dialogue differ from Dickens's novel and are the original creation of its authors. You are at liberty, if it strikes your fancy, to write another musical based on *Oliver Twist*, but you cannot use the variations from Dickens's story that the authors of *Oliver* created, unless they are absolutely necessary to the task and unavoidable.

If the derivative work you make is of a work still

subject to copyright, much the same rules apply. Your copyright in your derivative work covers only your own inventions, variations, and additions. You have no right to authorize someone else to use those parts of your derivative work that you have taken from the original.[13] For example, if you obtain a license to create a new edition of a copyrighted book, you can permit someone to publish your version as such, for that is implicit in your license, but you have no right to publish separately those parts of it that you took from the original. Nor can you, without authority from the original copyright owner, permit someone else to make yet another revised edition of what is not original with you. Furthermore, when the copyright term of the original work runs out, everything in your work that you took from the original goes into the public domain, and only what you yourself have created will remain protected. The converse is also true: If a derivative work loses its copyright, the copyright of the original remains unaffected.

Tracing a work through its derivative forms can be like tagging migratory animals. Take the example of the movie *South Pacific*. It started out as a collection of short stories by James Michener. Next, several of the stories were combined and adapted into a musical by Rodgers and Hammerstein. Then the musical was rewritten as a screenplay, and the screenplay was made into a movie. There were thus three layers of derivative works, each cutting old material and adding new. And the movie producer had three different copyrights to worry about: the novel, the musical, and the screenplay. The movie could not be made without derivative work licenses covering all three previous forms.

Expression
The third requirement of copyrightability is that the work be "expression" and not "idea." It is an old truism in copyright law that you cannot copyright an idea but only your expression of it: ideas, like facts, are in the public domain. For example, a literary critic who publishes a new theory of the structure of the novel cannot obtain a copyright in that theory; he can copyright only his written expression of that theory. A thief may steal his theory with impunity if the thief expresses the theory in his own words, and the thief, scurrilous though he may be, can obtain a new copyright in his own written work. Perhaps the first author should have an action for unfair competition if no attribution is made, given the nature of scholarly competition. But such a doctrine, which would be separate from copyright, has yet to develop.

A simple example like this one of literary criticism may make the rule itself seem simple. It is not. In fact it is riddled with ambiguities. What, for example, is a musical "idea" and how is it separable from musical "expression"? How basic must a plot become, how stripped of embellishment, before it ceases to be the writer's own copyrightable expression and becomes mere "idea"? No one really knows the answers to these questions, though many a court has formulated an all-embracing theory, only to see it discarded by the next court.

The rule that an idea cannot be copyrighted has an interesting corollary: copyright in the expression of an idea will not be enforced so as to prevent other people from putting the idea to practical use. This principle was first stated in the last century, in the case of *Baker v. Selden,* which involved a book on accounting techniques.[14] The book described a system of bookkeeping and, as illustration of it, contained a page ruled into columns appropriate for the system.

When another publisher, impressed by the system, printed and sold copies of the ruled page—without any explanatory material—the original author brought suit.

In a decision that has continued to reverberate through the case law ever since, the Supreme Court held for the defendant. It said that if a copyrighted work describes a system or process, copyright does not prevent anyone else from making whatever printed works are necessary to use that system. To hold otherwise, the Court said, would be to treat the copyright like a patent.

It is important to understand the limits of this principle. *Baker v. Selden* does not stand for the proposition that blank forms cannot be copyrighted. It does mean, though, that forms will not be protected if protection would prevent other people from using the system they embody. Nor does *Baker v. Selden* apply to forms that are purely arbitrary in their content, such as the answer sheets for copyrighted tests.[15]

In recent years the rule of *Baker v. Selden* has been applied to insurance contracts and other works that have a business or commercial use. The rule is that if a certain order of words is the only reasonable way, or one of only a few reasonable ways, of putting an idea to use, that precise order of words will be protected only narrowly or not at all.[16] This is sometimes referred to as the "merger doctrine," because idea and expression are seen as merged.

Under certain circumstances an idea may be protected before publication by an agreement to treat it as confidential. (Confidentiality is part of the law of trade secrets and is not a part of the copyright law.) If you wish to submit an idea for a work or an advertising program or something of the sort, make every effort to get a written or at least oral agreement in advance from whomever you wish to submit it to that it will be treated in confidence and paid for if used. In the absence of such an agreement, the other person will probably not be obligated to pay you. You will have only yourself to blame if you blurt out your idea without getting this protection.

If you are submitting an idea to your employer, the nature of your job may determine whether you have any rights in it. Try to clarify this in advance with the employer. When submitting an idea, whether as an insider or an outsider, be sure also that it is worked out in reasonable detail and described clearly in words or pictures. The vaguer or more general the idea, the less likely will courts impose liability on the user.

Scope of Copyright

Once the three basic requirements of fixation, originality, and expression are met, the law's protection, though not universal, is extremely broad. Almost any kind of artistic work or work that communicates a message in any tangible medium can be copyrighted. The statute specifically lists literary works (a term that means practically any printed work), musical works (including accompanying words), dramatic works (including accompanying music), pantomimes, choreographic works, "pictorial, graphic, and sculptural works" (in other words any visual work, whether two- or three-dimensional), sound recordings, motion pictures and all other audiovisual works—and this list is not complete.[17] None of these categories implies artistic merit; the telephone directory is considered a "literary work," and roadmaps are "graphic works."[18]

Performances of works are not regarded as works themselves until they are fixed, on tape or film, as sound recordings or audiovisual works. They are therefore not protected by copyright law until that time. This does not mean that someone can film or record a performance without the performer's permission, for that is forbidden by other laws.[19] Whether it means that someone can imitate that performer's interpretation or style is a matter on which the courts have not agreed. In a recent case on the subject, Bette Midler was able to stop the use of television commercials in which another singer imitated her voice and style.[20]

Although the law does not require that a work have artistic merit, certain works nonetheless do stand outside its shelter, in the cold drizzle of uncopyrightability. They are excluded for one of two reasons: either they are trivial, or they are utilitarian.

In the first category fall, for example, titles and slogans, simple designs, and minor variations on works already in the public domain.[21] Titles and slogans can be protected to some extent by federal trademark law and by state laws against unfair competition and misappropriation; a title, for example, will be protected by those laws if it has acquired such a reputation in the public mind that the use of it by someone else would amount to taking a free ride on the first user's popularity.[22] This protection, though, exists entirely apart from copyright and is not available for most items that are excluded from copyright on the grounds of triviality. Ballroom or discotheque dance steps, for example, are not considered to rise to the level of choreographic works within the meaning of the copyright statute and are unlikely to find protection under any other legal doctrine.[23]

The exclusion of utilitarian works is considerably less simple a concept. A typeface is not copyrightable as a pictorial or graphic work because Congress feels that typefaces are fundamentally utilitarian—that is, the purpose of their existence is to produce other things. There is every reason to believe that this interpretation applies equally well to calligraphic alphabets not intended as typefaces. An illuminated letter is clearly copyrightable as a pictorial work, but someone's personal variation of the uncial alphabet would probably not be. Anyone could use that alphabet in making other works, although the calligrapher's actual writings could not be printed and sold without permission.

As one explores the concept that utilitarian aspects of design are not copyrightable, it grows more difficult to find one's way. Congress has said that elements of utilitarian articles that "can be identified separately from the useful article as such"—that is, elements that are not functional—are copyrightable.[24] One almost needs training in Platonic philosophy to be able to make this sort of distinction. One is being asked, in essence, to discuss the lampness of a lamp, the tableness of a table. I bid you look up from this book for a moment at the lamp beneath which you are reading and identify those parts of its design that may clearly be segregated from its functional requirements. If your lamp is by Tiffany, your task will be relatively easy; if, on the other hand, it is made in the Scandinavian style, the problem is rather more challenging. One court has recently held that design elements that are influenced to any degree by utilitarian considerations should be denied copyright.[25] This is an effective, if draconian, resolution.

Does this mean that if a lamp cannot be copyrighted, a drawing of it cannot be either? Not so. Even a drawing by a lamp designer, made not as an end in itself but solely as a prelude to manufacture, is copyrightable as a pictorial work because it is not in itself a useful article but only teaches how to make one. No one may publish copies of the drawing without the designer's permission. However, the copyright does not prevent someone from actually making a lamp that embodies the functional parts portrayed in the drawing. (Here again you hear the echo of *Baker v. Selden*.) The designer's right to control manufacture based on his drawing extends only to those parts of his drawing that depict nonfunctional things.[26]

Architectural works present a special difficulty. An architect's plans, like any other drawings, are copyrightable as pictorial or graphic works. No one may copy or publish those drawings without the architect's permission. However, so far as the functional, utilitarian elements depicted by those drawings are concerned, anyone who sees the blueprints can erect a building incorporating those elements, and the architect cannot stop him.[27]

What about the building itself, once it is built? As a rule buildings are not copyrightable, and one architect or builder may copy another's building so long as no tracing, photocopying, or other reproduction of the original plans is involved. But the law does provide that "nonfunctional" or "monumental" structures are copyrightable as sculptural works.[28] What do *nonfunctional* and *monumental* mean? The pyramids are now regarded as monuments, but when they were built they were perceived as functional. The Committee Report for the Copyright Act says that copyright will not cover elements of shape in a building that are "conceptually inseparable from the utilitarian aspects of the structure," a distinction that may prove as difficult to make in practice as in the example of the Scandinavian lamp.[29]

Plots and Characters

In works that tell stories, the coverage afforded by copyright is broader than one might think, primarily because more and more things that long ago were considered merely ideas have come to be regarded as expression. For example, the plot of a novel is covered by the novel's copyright, at least to the extent that it is original with the author. The courts have developed the ingenious theory that a plot is an "arrangement of ideas" and that an arrangement of ideas amounts, magically, to "expression."[30] From a philosophical or logical point of view, this is probably a falsehood, but nonetheless it is the law.

What about characters? Here again the law gives protection to what might at first seem to be an idea. Indeed similarity of characters is often the principal battleground when one author sues another for plagiarism. But there is one unusually perplexing problem with characters: who owns them? (You may as well resign yourself early to one of the facts of life of copyright law: no principle is fixed or firm, self-defining or self-limiting. If you are commonsensical, this will cause you frequent exasperation, but on the other hand common sense will also tend to get you out of the mazes into which pure logic leads.)

This problem of characters arose in a case involving *The Maltese Falcon*.[31] After selling the story to Warner Brothers, Dashiell Hammett wrote several more stories about his detective hero, Sam Spade. Warner Brothers took him to court, claiming that he had violated the terms of his contract of sale and that the character, Sam Spade, was their exclusive property.

It might have been enough for the court to construe the contract in Hammett's favor and to hold that he had not in fact sold Warner Brothers his rights in Sam Spade. The court did this, but it did not let the matter rest there. It went on to consider whether a character, as such, could even be copyrighted, and concluded that it could not, unless it constituted the story being told. (Emma in Jane Austen's novel might be an example of the latter case.) Its opinion was that characters like Sam Spade are a writer's stock-in-trade and that the activities or words of a character in a particular story are copyrightable but not the character as such. The court characterized an author's ownership of a character as property of a different sort—property that is protected by ordinary legal rules, not by copyright law.

This case has been nothing if not controversial. Commentators note that courts have often found (or denied) infringement of literary works by comparing their characters, thus suggesting that characters are indeed covered by copyright. And yet on closer analysis perhaps these characters fit the formula of the Spade case, as the story (or elements of the story) being told. The character who stands apart from the story, however, has an ancient lineage. From Genji to Sherlock Holmes, the world's literature is rich with heroes (and with villains like Professor Moriarty) whose identity builds over the span of many tales. Can there be any doubt that if Conan Doyle were our contemporary he could sue someone who created a detective with Holmes's characteristics, even if the new detective had a different name? And yet the character of Holmes does not reside in any one of Conan Doyle's stories. Assignment of copyright in any one of them would certainly not assign the rights to Holmes the character.

In the practical world people need not agonize over this issue. Publishers and movie producers who want the rights to characters usually include them specifically in their contracts. And conversely people who wish to retain the rights to their characters should specify as much in their contracts.

Nonetheless, if the Sam Spade case is still good law, its implications are far-reaching, particularly under the new law. How long does this unusual property right in characters last? Does it vanish when the author dies, or can he bequeath it to his children? Can he bequeath it to someone who has no connection at all with his copyrights? Could Hammett, for example, have bequeathed his rights in Sam Spade to Lillian Hellman, and would Hammett's children and publishers then have been powerless to stop her from writing books about Sam Spade? (The court never faced these problems; I would not venture to guess how a court might decide them in the future.)

The final problem of this case is that it may mean that a sale by an author of his "property" in a character is not protected by the provision in the new law that permits an author to terminate (revoke) a transfer of copyright. I shall deal with termination at length in chapter 3; I raise the point now only to underscore the dangers presented.

I should add that most of these issues do not arise where cartoon or other visual characters are concerned. Mickey Mouse and his colleagues are clearly protected by copyright as works of visual art.

Computer Programs

Many principles of copyright are being put to the test as courts struggle with questions concerning computer programs. Programs are eligible for copyright, but there is considerable confusion about what such a copyright protects or should protect.

For the moment the law is that a computer program is protected not only in source code form but in object code form as well. This is true even if the object code is embedded in the computer, as is the case with operating system software.[32] (Source code is the version of a program that is written in FORTRAN, PASCAL, C, or any of the other so-called computer languages. The source code of a program is not intelligible to a layman, but can be easily read and understood by experts. Object code, on the other hand, is the machine-readable form of a program, whether in tape, disk, or other form, and is intelligible for the most part only to the machine it is put into, not to humans. Operating system software is the set of instructions that governs the computer's thought processes, so to speak.) I say "for the moment" because there are real difficulties in this doctrine that have yet to be resolved.

At the time that this sensitive area was being studied by the National Commission on New Technological Uses of Copyrighted Works (CONTU), most Commission members felt that object code was merely a copy of the source code and should be protected by copyright. In a vigorous dissent, however, the novelist John Hersey and others protested that an object code, although it is an embodiment of the source code, functions solely as a part of the computer, is not intended to communicate to human beings, and should not be protected by copyright.[33] Thus the dispute centered on what the copyright law means when it defines a "copy" as "a material object in which a work is fixed by any method now known or later developed, and from which the work can be perceived, reproduced, or otherwise communicated, either directly or with the aid of a machine or device." The majority of the Commission took the view that the object code of a program was a copy because, theoretically, the source code could be printed out from it. The fact is, however, that that is not the purpose of object code, and indeed the last thing any program vendor wants is for his program to be deciphered; most try (however futilely) to encrypt or otherwise protect their object codes from ever being "read" and understood.

In my opinion the dissent held the higher ground, so far as logic is concerned. But logic is not the only force at work here; CONTU and the courts have, whether consciously or not, acted partly out of fear that not to extend copyright protection to object code will open the gates to the Japanese or Taiwanese invader. Certainly that fear is widespread in the computer industry. Many computer people will, if pressed, admit that copyright doesn't fit very well onto object code, but, they say, patent protection is expensive and time-consuming to obtain, and most programs have only a short commercial life.

The problem with the current state of the law is that granting copyright protection to things like operating system software—to pick the most blatant example—is in effect granting a long-term patentlike monopoly in the machine itself, without requiring the inventor to meet the standards of patentability. This is not healthy for the economy, nor in the long run for the law either. A better solution might be to enact a special statute for software, combining elements of patent and copyright.

Accepting that copyright applies to software, we must somehow distinguish the "expression" in a program from the "idea." A program is fundamentally a series of instructions directing a computer to perform certain analytic or other functions. If the problem to be solved is a difficult one, writing the program requires great skill and creativity, and, we say at a gut level, this effort deserves protection. But how do we protect those instructions without actually protecting the process they embody? In the precomputer age instructions for doing something, even something as arbitrary as playing a game, were narrowly limited in their copyrights.[34] CONTU considered this question and decided that for any given data-processing problem there were a great number of possible programming solutions. At a certain level of specificity, they said, the choice of computer instructions constitutes the "expression" of the general solution or algorithm, which in turn constitutes the idea.[35]

If this strikes you as disingenuous, I am inclined to agree. A process is no less a process just because it is set out in more detail or is chosen from a group of processes that have the same end result. CONTU's analysis likens a program to the plot of a novel, in which the arrangement of ideas can constitute expression. But the specifics of a plot are themselves a commentary on human life and as such constitute part of the novel's end result; it cannot be said that two plots, in their details, are merely two ways of getting from A to B, because the author's choice of details helps define and describe the world he is writing about. Furthermore, and perhaps more important, a novelist sitting down to write is not limited in his choice of plot, setting, or any of those other things that comprise expression by the need to arrive at B. He has the whole world from which to choose his details, and if the choice leads him ultimately to C, so much the better: the muse is at work. In other words the novelist's choices are arbitrary, dictated only by imagination. A computer programmer, on the other hand, cannot choose details at random but must always have his eye on B, and is judged on his skill by how quickly and efficiently he gets there. ("Efficiently"—is that a word compatible with copyright?) Still the CONTU theory has some validity, if only because there is no clear alternative.

Unfortunately, many programmers believe that the true commercial value of a program lies in the algorithm, not in the programming details. Any good programmer, they say, can take a piece of software and, using its basic structure, come up with a program that will do the same things in somewhat different ways. This puts us squarely in a dilemma, for we cannot protect against that sort of rearrangement without in effect protecting the ideas of the program.

Some recent cases have plunged head first into this crevasse. Perhaps most controversial is *Whelan Associates, Inc. v. Jaslow Dental Laboratories, Inc.*,[36] in which it was held that the "overall structure" of a computer program could be protected by copyright. Addressing the idea-expression dichotomy, the court said that the "idea" concerned was the idea of running a dental laboratory by using a computer, thus implying that everything in the program more specific than that constituted copyrightable expression. Not even CONTU would have praised such a holding. If copyright protects the "overall structure" of a program, is it not protecting the algorithm? It is not protecting the process or method of the program, both of which are specifically excluded from copyright by statute? The answers seem obvious, and yet one cannot safely predict how the law will evolve in this area. The case has been criticized, and another Court of Appeals has "declined to follow" it, although for a narrower reason than argued here.[37]

Given this unsettled state of the law, how should one protect software? The answer probably varies depending on the type of software. Despite the difficulty, delay, and expense of obtaining a patent, some software producers have found it desirable to do so. The coverage of a patent, although of shorter duration, is much broader than that of a copyright. The

Supreme Court has upheld the issuance of a patent where a computer program is the key part—indeed the only novel part—of a mechanical process.[38] Patents of this type are now granted without much controversy. Patent thus appears well suited to robotics, expert systems, and the like. Furthermore there appears to be a trend in the U.S. Patent Office toward granting patents to algorithms, even where there is little if any connection to patent's traditional realm of processes, devices, and machines. For example, a patent has been granted to the algorithm developed at Bell Labs that can be used for optimal routing of airplanes or telephone calls.[39] But patents are time-consuming to obtain and may turn out to have a high mortality rate in the courts. For many applications only copyright is appropriate.

Some who secure patents for their programs also secure copyright. The apparent conflict can perhaps be resolved by saying that patent protects the algorithm and structure of the program, whereas copyright protects the program at a more specific level. (Such a rationalization is questionable if *Whelan* is good law.) Thus when the seventeen-year patent term ends, copyright would continue to protect the specific instruction sequences of the program.

Yet for many software producers neither patent nor copyright is desirable. In fact, anyone planning to distribute software by one-on-one licensing would do well to follow common industry practice and rely primarily on trade-secret protection. This involves placing tight restrictions on the uses that the customer can make of the software, prohibiting disclosure to persons other than the licensee and its key employees, and requiring return or destruction of the software if for any reason the license is terminated. If you are marketing your software over the counter, trade-secret protection is of course not appropriate. In such a case copyright is probably the only alternative now available.

Another area of controversy in the application of copyright to software is the protection of the "look and feel" of a program. At issue is the user interface of a program, which consists primarily of the menus and other displays that appear on the screen and the order of keystrokes by which a user inputs and manipulates data.

Popular software begets imitation, and clever imitators can copy the user interface of a program without copying any underlying code. Such is the case with Lotus Development Corporation's popular spreadsheet program, 1-2-3, which has become the industry standard for financial spreadsheet software. In 1989 Lotus had a suit pending against two "clone" producers.

The threshold question presented by these look-and-feel cases is whether the screen displays are a separate work from the underlying code or both are parts of one unitary work. The U.S. Copyright Office has taken the position that if both the code and the display are produced by the same persons, they should be treated as two parts of a single work. In this the Office expressly disagreed with a prior District Court case on the point.[40]

Assuming the Copyright Office view prevails, it nonetheless seems likely that courts will judge the copyrightability of screen displays separately from that of the code. One court has already done so.[41] This means that a court may acknowledge copyright in the unitary work as a whole, but still find that the screen display element is not copyrightable, just as it might find a novel to be copyrightable as a whole, but deny copyright protection to various scenes or plot sequences. What sorts of screen displays, then, may be protected?

There can be little doubt that video-game screens are copyrightable, provided they contain a minimal level of original expression.[42] They are, in essence, animated cartoons.

But what about spreadsheet displays? Clone manufacturers argue that spreadsheets and accompanying menus, like the accounting sheets in *Baker v. Selden*, cannot be given copyright without granting a monopoly to Lotus in the financial planning techniques that the spreadsheets embody. This argument gains force when one considers that *1–2-3* is in fact the industry standard; so many businesses have recorded their data in *1–2-3* format that copyright in the format could create a virtual monopoly. By contrast, a court recently found that in the rather limited field of cost estimating, the available programs were radically different from each other in their screen displays. On this basis the court found plaintiff's screens to be copyrightable, and also the "flow" or sequencing of those screens.[43]

A related issue raised in the Lotus and other look-and-feel cases is the copyrightability of the keystrokes required of the user. Here I am extremely skeptical of the validity of copyright. Here the *Baker v. Selden* doctrine seems especially apposite, where the very method of *use* of the program is at stake.[44]

As the foregoing discussion may suggest, where computer software is concerned, we are dealing with something suspiciously like new wine and old bottles.

Works Created with the Aid of Computers

Can a work created by applying a computer program to a data base receive a copyright? A typical work of this sort might be a biblical concordance, created by feeding the Bible into a computer data bank and then applying it to a program designed to locate and arrange word correspondences. Although no case has yet raised the issue, there seems to be no reason why a work of this type should not be entitled to a copyright. Admittedly the computer is doing the bulk of the legwork, but this is only at the guidance of a human being. It is a tool, no matter how creative it may be. A certain degree of human will and intellectual labor is present in any computer product.

As intellectual production of this type becomes more and more common, some unusual problems of ownership will emerge. I shall deal with these in greater detail in the next chapter.

Mask Works

By an amendment to the Copyright Act in 1984, Congress granted a truncated form of copyright protection to the masks, so called, that are used to create semiconductor chips.[45] It was felt that these masks, being essentially unitarian works, would not receive protection without specific statutory language.

A mask lies somewhere between a design and a stencil, or perhaps more accurately it is both. In it the intricate circuitry of a semiconductor chip is cut, and through it laser light etches the circuitry design on the chip's silicon. Because of its inherently unitarian character, Congress has granted mask works a shorter term of protection and a narrower scope of rights than other works. And, interestingly, Congress has specifically authorized anyone to use the technology contained in a mask work, provided he obtains it by reverse engineering and does not merely copy the mask.[46]

2 Ownership

Copyright comes into existence at the moment of a work's creation, just as, in some theologies, the soul enters the body at birth. At that time ownership vests in the author or authors.

The word *author* has a special meaning in the copyright law. It is used regardless of the kind of work; writers, painters, sculptors, and composers are all authors. This usage indeed is almost universal—in other countries as a matter of convenience and in this country as a necessity. The Constitution, from which Congress derives its power to establish copyrights, speaks specifically of "authors" and "writings," and to extend the law's protection to nonliterary works, the courts have had to interpret these words broadly. However, *author* is not synonymous with *creator*, for in certain circumstances a person, or company, will be considered an author without lifting a creative finger. So what seems at first almost a frivolous question—Who is the author?—is in fact both complex and important.

Authorship

Only in a work by one individual acting on his own behalf is the answer to the question obvious. In the case, of say, a poem written by one person and set to music by another, it is anything but obvious. Three different relationships can exist between that poet and that composer. The first, in which the words and music are considered separately, can hardly even be called a relationship. The poet is the author of the words and may do what he likes with his poem; the composer is the author of the music and may do with the music anything that he pleases. In the absence of some exclusive licensing arrangement, the first composer cannot prevent another from making a new musical setting for the poem, and the first poet cannot prevent another from writing new words to fit the music. A singer who wants to perform such a song would have to buy the performance right in the poem from the poet and the performance right in the music from the composer.

It is also possible, and more common, for the poet and composer to be "joint authors," and for the song to be a "joint work." Joint authorship ranks among the more slippery principles of copyright law, and many courts and communities have grappled with it without achieving a clear victory. Intuitively we all know what a joint work is; it is, just as the statute says, a work "prepared by two or more authors with the intention that their contributions be merged into inseparable or interdependent parts of a unitary whole."[1] But what do these words mean? Do they mean that for a work to be a joint work, all of the authors must agree among themselves before any of them begins creating any part of the work? That would violate good sense. As one court said in a case under the old law,

Suppose, for example, that after Burnett had composed the music, expecting his wife to write the words, she had died or changed her mind about writing the lyrics, and Burnett had gone to [his publisher]

and asked him to find someone to write the words. We submit that no court would hold that the fact that when Burnett composed the music he expected his wife to write the words, would make the actual song any less a "joint work" of Burnett and the lyricist found by [his publishers].[2]

The force of this reasoning cannot be denied, and there seems no reason not to apply it to the new statute. As the House Report accompanying the new statute makes clear, the "intention" on which the law is focused is the intention with which the author's contribution was created.[3] And as the Burnett case makes clear, the intention need not be *mutual* among the authors; it is sufficient that each author have intended that his product be merged with others. Thus even if a lyricist dies before finding a composer, when a composer is finally found, the resulting work will be a joint work.

What is less clear is whether anything is gained by focusing on intention where the contributions are inseparable. Take, for example, the case of a mystery writer who, when she is halfway done, decides to bring in a collaborator to finish her newest work. Their contributions are inseparable, and the work is inescapably a joint work; no possible alternative designation exists. Now suppose instead that the first writer dies, leaving an unfinished manuscript. Her executor finds another writer willing to finish the book. Should the resulting work not be considered a joint work? The deceased author certainly intended that there be only one work, yet technically she did not intend that her efforts be merged with those of any other writer. The alternative is to consider the unfinished manuscript a completed work for copyright purposes and the finished product a derivative work with separate copyright. This seems absurd, but one cannot be sure it is incorrect.

Where joint authorship exists, it creates a hybrid sort of ownership. Joint authors are not like joint owners of a house, with the last survivor taking the whole title. Instead they are regarded as "tenants in common." This means that each of them owns an undivided share of the entire work and can bequeath that share to his own heirs. This share is not necessarily equal, for the authors can slice the pie unevenly if they so choose.[4] Unlike someone who owns land as a tenant in common, however, a joint author cannot sue to divide the property. Instead, because ownership is theoretically undivided, each joint author can grant rights in the work without consulting the others. (If he does so, he will have to account to his fellow authors for their shares of the profits.) Yet by the same token a grant by any one joint author will not prevent any of the other joint authors from making an identical sale to someone else. For this reason purchasers generally insist on getting all of the authors to sign the contract.

Outside the United States the rule is stricter: a grant will not be effective unless signed by all joint authors, and anyone contemplating foreign distribution of a work should insist on obtaining all signatures.[5]

Works Made for Hire

I have discussed so far two possible relationships between persons whose creative efforts are in some manner connected. The first is that they are merely independent authors combining their independent creations; the second is that they are joint authors. A third possible relationship is that one of them is an employee of the other, in which case the resulting work is a "work made for hire." Works made for hire have a different copyright term from that of most other works, and they are the only works for which an author has no statutory right to terminate a transfer. (See the discussion of termination of rights in chapter 3.) The author of a work made for hire is the person who does the "hiring"; the creator has no rights whatever in the work.

The most obvious examples of works made for hire are newspapers, movies, dictionaries, and other works that we think of as created, in a sense, by the companies that publish them. These companies have staffs of full-time writers and artists who work specifically on these products.

The rule is broader though. An employer is considered the author of anything written by an employee within the scope of his employment. Thus when a scientist in a research laboratory writes a report on her work for her supervisor, the laboratory is the author of the report.

How can you tell if a person is an employee, within the meaning of the law? The clear-cut example is the full-time staff writer, who is an employee in every sense of the word. But what about someone who is commissioned to create a specific work, is paid by the job—or not paid at all—and then moves on? The Supreme Court has recently attempted to answer that question, with results that may not be entirely desirable.

First, a word of background. Under pre-1978 law it was generally held that one who commissioned a work became the "author" and copyright owner. This was a judge-made rule, based on what courts perceived as the legitimate expectations of the parties. For example, commissioned portraits were works for hire, and the copyright belonged to the purchaser instead of the painter.[6] Where a company paid someone to develop an advertisement, a court would grant copyright to the company, believing that any other result would be unfair.[7]

The old statute was rather cursory on this question of what constitutes "for hire." By contrast the new statute goes into it at some length. It sets up two categories of work for hire: on the one hand, work created by an employee "within the scope of his or her employment"; on the other hand, a specifically ordered or commissioned work if it falls within one of nine clearly defined categories and if the parties have agreed in writing to treat the work as made for hire.

The question then arose whether by this new language Congress intended to limit the work-for-hire doctrine, in cases of commissioned materials, to works that fall within the nine defined categories and are the subject of written agreements, or whether in some cases a commissioned person could still be viewed as, in some broader sense, an employee.

The first major case on this point came up from New York to the Second Circuit. It involved authorship of certain statuettes, and the evidence showed that the people who commissioned the work had actively participated in its creation, giving detailed instructions on various design issues. The Second Circuit held that even though the commissioned artisans were not employees in the legal sense, they had acted under the "direction and control" of the commissioning party and thus should be regarded as employees for work-for-hire purposes.[8] This rule was subsequently followed by a number of other courts and was extended to cases where a commissioning party had the *right* to supervise and control, even though the right might never have been exercised.[9]

All was tranquil, then, until the Fifth Circuit rejected this doctrine in the case of *Easter Seals Society for Crippled Children v. Playboy Enterprises.*[10] The facts are less titillating (and less one-sided) than the name of the case might suggest; at issue was ownership of some film footage of jazz musicians that had been made at the request of the Easter Seals Society for use in a promotional broadcast.

The Fifth Circuit carried out what might be termed archaeology on the statute, interpreting it in the light of the various drafts it had gone through, remarks of legislators, and the like. It decided that although "employee" did not mean only persons on a payroll, the term did exclude independent contractors who were merely subject to direction and control. An "employee" had to be either an employee in the strictest sense or at least someone acting as "agent" for the other party. (At common law, contrary to popular usage, an "agent" is neither a spy nor a broker but any person who acts on another's behalf, rather than his own.) To determine agency, the court suggested looking to the law of personal injury: if one would be held liable for a physical injury caused by a commissioned artist, one would be that artist's employer for copyright purposes.

Following this reasoning, the District of Columbia Circuit held, in the case that ultimately went on to the Supreme Court, that a statue belonged to the sculptor even though the charity that commissioned the sculpture had contributed portions of it and made far more than cursory stipulations about its design.[11] The D.C. Circuit Court went so far as to suggest that the commissioning charity and the sculptor might be joint authors—an idea neither party had suggested or, we may suppose, would happily endorse.

Not to be outdone, the Ninth Circuit, sitting in California, subsequently held that only works produced by actual salaried employees could be works made for hire, unless they fell within one of the nine special categories and were subject to written agreements.[12]

The end result of all this judicial activity was that, as of 1989, who owned copyright in a commissioned work depended on what circuit's jurisdiction you were under. At this point the Supreme Court stepped in and delivered a definitive ruling. The Supreme Court upheld the District of Columbia Circuit's view.[13]

Though it may be idle now to complain, all sides in this dispute have been guilty of the kind of entrail reading, known euphemistically as "statutory history," that other countries do not allow courts to indulge in when interpreting a law. All sides are victims of a Congress that seems incapable of saying what it means.

All sides have also overstated the virtues of their positions. The Fifth and D.C. Circuits, and now the Supreme Court, have claimed that their rule would promote certainty by adopting a "bright line" definition of employee. But nothing could be further from the truth. As I have noted, the D.C. Circuit suggested that joint ownership should apply where an artist is not an employee but the commissioning party makes substantial input into the work. The Supreme Court has followed this lead, and the case has now been remanded to the trial court for further proceedings on this very point. Of what benefit is such a Solomonic decision? Neither the artist nor the patron can grant an exclusive license to a publisher, and no one in the real world will ever pay much for a nonexclusive license. The result is not certainty but stalemate. Perhaps the parties will settle their differences and work out some *modus vivendi*. But perhaps they will not, and the work will never see the circulation it deserves. The law should avoid violently yoking together people who do not intend to be yoked.

Some groups representing the interests of authors have hailed this decision as a great victory. I am not convinced. It does unquestionably place on commissioning parties the burden of obtaining written agreements. An advertiser, for example, will need a written assignment of copyright to own the ads it commissions. Many deals that have traditionally been done on a handshake will require new legalisms. Those already consummated are now open to revision, because the Supreme Court's ruling is retroactive to January 1, 1976.

But if the commissioning parties have the bargaining power, they will usually manage to extract by contract what the old law gave them by right. The only right an author cannot contract away is the right of termination after thirty-five years (discussed in chapter 3); this right is meaningful only to the most significant works of art or letters. It has no relevance in the fields where the work-for-hire rules actually operate: commercial photography, computer software, and so forth. So what the new rule has accomplished, where commissioning parties are alert, is to stimulate a lot of new paperwork, and where they are not alert, is to create a trap into which they can stumble.

Even on its own terms the "bright line" rule adopted by the Supreme Court is anything but self-defining. As noted, it imports into copyright the law of agency, a strange new bedfellow. Treatises have been written about agency; treatises are not written about things that are nice and neat. How are we to know whether someone fits the "agent" profile? If the only control exercised by the commissioning party is in the creative process itself, we are caught in a tautology, and no matter how pervasive that control may be, it may be insufficient to save the commissioning party. The Supreme Court has not absolutely ruled out the possibility that such a relationship could be "for hire." It has, however, stated that the following factors (and perhaps others as well) should be assessed when determining whether an agency relationship exists, and it has given no guidance as to how they should be weighed. I list these factors with some observations as to their application:

• *The skill required* Presumably a highly skilled artisan is less likely to be an employee than a mere paper-pusher.

• *The source of the tools and materials used to create the work* Where these are owned by the commissioning party, its case is stronger.

• *The duration of the relationship* A one-time job is less likely to be a for-hire relationship than one of long standing in which various works are created.

• *Whether the commissioning party has the right to assign additional projects to the creative party.*

• *Who determines when and how long the creative party works.*

• *The method of payment* A flat fee (or better yet a royalty) will be most favorable to the creative party, and an hourly fee will be most favorable to the commissioning party.

• *Who decides what assistants will be hired, and who pays them.*

• *Whether the work is in the ordinary line of business of the commissioning party* The doll factory that commissions a new doll will fare better than the automobile dealership that commissions a music video.

• *Whether the creative party is in business on its own.*

• *Whether the creative party receives employee benefits such as health insurance from the commissioning party.*

• *The tax treatment of the creative party* For example, if the commissioning party pays FICA and withholding on an artist's earnings, it is more likely to be the copyright "author" than if the artist pays self-employment taxes.

It all begins to sound a lot like Justice Potter Stewart's test for pornography: "I know it when I see it." It runs the risk of yielding irreconcilable results as courts all over the country decide cases ad hoc. It certainly underscores the desirability of reducing every contract to writing, and specifically allocating copyright ownership.

And the final problem, which the Supreme Court's decision fails to address, is that at one level or another the parties' rights are always going to be ad hoc unless *everything* is written down. This is good for the legal profession but not for the polity. An example may help to illustrate this.

The example is unfortunately a common one, and because the Supreme Court's decision has retroactive effect, many cases like it are apt to pop up in the near future. Suppose Green commissions Brown to create a work of some sort, and it does not qualify as a work made for hire. What rights do Green and Brown actually have in the work? If it is a portrait, for example, Green obviously has ownership of the portrait itself and thus has a limited right to display it publicly.[14] Green does not own any other rights in it.

Suppose, though, that the work is something Green intends to use, such as advertising material. Fairness would dictate that Green have a nonexclusive license to publish the work, to display or perform it, and to make new versions or other derivative works based on it.[15] However, does Brown have to

give Green access to the printing plates and negatives, or master tapes, so that Green can reproduce
the work conveniently? The statute does not say so,
and neither does any reported case. Under the old
law it was usually held that a commissioning party
had the copyright and thus was entitled to the plates,
negatives, and similar material.[16] The issue rarely
arose. Under the new law, however, there is no such
easy way out.

Would Brown, the commissioned creator of the ad,
be at liberty to revise the same advertising materials
for the use of another client? Logically he ought to
be, but it is not at all clear that this is so. The law
might seek to imply a restriction on Brown's exercise
of his rights, although this is problematic, given the
primacy of the copyright law over state law doctrines
of equity.[17] So we are back to where we started, with
an emphasis on the parties' states of mind—the very
thing the bright liners claim to be avoiding.

Therefore it bears repeating: Reduce your deals to
writing. Try to be explicit about copyright ownership
and about any uses or restrictions on use that might
some day become important.

If you are considered an employee, however that
term is defined, can you arrange for your work not to
be considered "for hire"? Unfortunately not. The
most you can do in advance is agree either that certain types of work will not be in the scope of employment or that even if the employer is to be the author,
you will still own the rights, or certain specific rights,
in the work. This amounts to a transfer in advance of
copyright ownership. The first type of agreement
may be written or oral, but written is more reliable.
The later type must be in writing and signed by both
the employer and the employee; otherwise the agree-

ment will be only a nonexclusive license to the employee.[18]

Under the old law this was not so. Before publication an author's entire copyright could be transferred orally, and this applied in the work-for-hire context as well.[19] By a handshake an employer and employee could effectively waive the work-for-hire rule. Even now the formality of requiring *both* signatures applies only to agreements between an employer and employee made in advance of creation of the work. After the work is in fact created, the normal rules for transfer of copyright apply. (See chapter 3.)

Returning to the subject of specially commissioned works—as noted, the law provides that certain types of commissioned works may be treated as works made for hire, regardless of the lack of supervision and control. These are:

• A contribution to a movie or other audiovisual work.

• A contribution to a periodical or other collective work.

• A translation.

• A supplementary work, that is, a work that is somehow auxiliary to the main work—for example, an illustration, an illustrative map or chart, editorial notes, a musical arrangement, a bibliography, a foreword, an index, and so forth—but only if it is subordinate to the main work. For example, illustrations that are of equivalent importance to the text will not qualify as subordinate works.

• A compilation, that is, a work created by collecting and assembling data or preexisting materials; an example would be an anthology, a hotel guide, or a racing chart.

• An instructional text.

• A test.

- Answer material for a test.
- An atlas.

For any of these commissioned works to be a work made for hire, the creator and whoever commissions the creator must agree that this will be so. The agreement must be in writing and signed by both of them. The law does not require in so many words that the contract has to say, "This work will be a work made for hire," but there is little doubt that that is what it means. A court is likely to interpret any language less explicit than this in the opposite way. Even if the contract says "A hires B to do such-and-such," a court may well believe that the word *hires* was used loosely as a synonym for *commissions.* The phrase *work made for hire* is a legal term and ought to be used wherever that is the intent.

By the same token any agreement that a person who is doing work for hire will have any exclusive rights in that work must also be in writing and signed by both parties.[20]

To be commissioned, a work must be done at the request of the person for whom it is done. Nevertheless some magazine publishers send to authors who have submitted unsolicited manuscripts contracts that say "This work will be a work made for hire." This is illogical and ineffective; at most, such a contract will be interpreted as a transfer of copyright ownership from the author to the magazine. On the other hand, if a work truly is commissioned, nothing says the written agreement to consider it a work for hire may not be signed after the work is done. For safety's sake, though, it probably should be signed before or as soon afterward as possible.

There is another interesting and potentially important twist in the law governing these special categories of commissioned works. The statute permits them to be considered works made for hire only if they are "specially ordered or commissioned for use as" a contribution to a collective work, a translation, or whatever. What if the commissioned work is not used in the way originally intended? For example, suppose that a drawing is commissioned to be used as a contribution to a periodical, but the publisher decides instead to use it as an illustration for a book, that is, as a supplementary work. Will the publisher still be considered the author? The law remains untested, and the matter is pure speculation, but it is a possibility to consider. People commissioning works should specify in the contract that those works may be used in any way the commissioning party thinks appropriate.

Authorship of Works Created with the Aid of Computers

As noted in chapter 1, a computer should properly be viewed as a tool of its user, so that the author of its output is the user of the system, not the copyright owner of the software. This logic may lead to problems, however, where a computer-made work is the result of human teamwork. If the members of the team are employees of a common employer, the employer will be the author of any work created, because of the work-for-hire doctrine. If, however, the team members come together voluntarily, whether they may be considered joint authors depends on their roles in the process.

I will take up again my example of a biblical concordance. Suppose Smith, Jones, and Brown enter into an agreement to produce a concordance, with Smith taking charge of developing the program, Jones compiling the database, and Brown inputting the program and processing the data. There would seem to be no question but that all three are joint authors of whatever is ultimately produced. But a strict reading of the statute does not permit such an interpretation. It requires that contributions be merged into inseparable or interdependent parts of the unitary whole. And the computer program is separate from any printout the computer makes; it remains intact, unchanged. Thus it would be illogical to say that the program is an "inseparable or inter-dependent part" of the printout, and illogical to call Smith, the author of the program, a joint author.

This reasoning may soothe those who purchase software for research purposes; it would certainly be unfair to expect them to divide their profits with the software retailer. But it wreaks havoc with enter-prises such as that of Smith, Jones, and Brown and forces Smith to resort to contract, or to partnership or trust law, for protection of his rights. Nonetheless that appears to be the law, and persons finding them-selves in Smith's position should seek contractual protection.[21]

These arguments apply with equal force to Jones, the creator of the database. We have thus excluded from the team of would-be joint authors both the software designer and the database assembler. Nor does there seem to be any way around this result, short of changing the law so that in every case the author of a computer program or database is a joint author of the end product, a change that would have a devastating impact on the software industry.

U.S. Government Works

One special variant of the work-for-hire rule relates to works of the U.S. Government. The law denies copyright to works "prepared by an officer or em-ployee of the United States Government as part of that person's official duties."[22] (These works may nonetheless receive copyright protection in other countries.[23]) By implication it seems probable that if a government officer or employee, working within the scope of his official duties, jointly authors a work with a private citizen, the private citizen will own the entire copyright and have no obligation beyond the terms of his contract to share any of the profits with the government. Will the government have any rights? It is impossible to say, for the issue has never been tried.

Problems arise in defining a person's official duties. The well-publicized lawsuits involving President Nixon's and Henry Kissinger's tapes and memoranda are only the most sensational. By and large the "scope-of-employment" test will work here as with other works for hire.[24] Unlike a private employer, though, the Government probably cannot waive its claim to authorship and thereby vest copyright in its employee or officer.

Authorship of Compilations

The term *compilation,* as used in the copyright law, covers any kind of work that assembles facts or brings together a number of independently created works. It includes directories, dictionaries, racing forms, and the like. It also includes the vast category of works known as "collective works": magazines, anthologies, and so on. It does not include works where the elements collected are artistically fused, as in the case of a collage or a poem like *The Waste Land.* The author of a compilation is the person who does the compiling. The copyright in a compilation covers only the arrangement and selection of material.

Divisibility

The principles of authorship determine who owns copyright at the time a work is first fixed in tangible form. At that point a property right comes into being and may be transferred to others. At that point also the principle of divisibility comes into play.

A copyright is in reality a bundle of rights, each of which may be exploited separately. These rights are: to reproduce the work, to distribute it to the public, to perform it publicly, to display it publicly, and to create derivative works based on it. The author may transfer any one or more of them without transferring the others. The owner or exclusive licensee of any of these rights is, with respect to that right, a "copyright owner." He is like a tenant who can sublet to a third person and collect rent from the subtenant.

The divisibility principle goes further than this, though, for each of these five rights can in turn be carved up in a hundred ways. A novelist need not give a publisher the entire publication right to her novel. She may give one publisher the hardcover rights and another publisher the paperback rights. A playwright need not sell to a producer his entire performance right; he may give the stage right to one producer and the television right to another. Rights can be carved up geographically and chronologically as well. There is in fact no end to the number of possible subsidiary rights, although some of them are more appropriate to certain kinds of work than to others. And any of those licensees, such as the television producer, is considered an owner of the work, to the extent of his license, as long as the license is exclusive.[25]

It is important to remember that copyright in a work is separate from the physical object. The person who owns a work of art, for example, does not necessarily own copyright in it.[26] All he owns is the right to display it publicly, and even that right does not extend to display by means of television broadcast. Furthermore, if the object is a movie or other audiovisual work, he can display publicly only one frame at a time.[27]

This means that the author of a work retains copyright even if the work itself is sold or given away. There is one major gap in this rule, however. Although the author theoretically owns the right to copy the work, nothing in the law requires the owner to give the author access to the actual object. An artist who has sold a canvas may find the right to copy it a rather empty privilege.

Community Property

A special problem of ownership affects those who live in states that treat property acquired during marriage as belonging equally to husband and wife. Is a copyright acquired after a marriage subject to this so-called "community property" rule? One state court, in California, has so held, reasoning that although federal law vests copyright in the author of a work, state law is free to transfer a share of that ownership to the author's spouse.[28] This is a somewhat controversial decision, and time will tell whether it remains good law.

Duration of Copyright

Authorship determines not only ownership of a copyright, but also its duration. The regular term is life of the author plus fifty years. In the case of a joint work, though, it is life of the last joint author to die plus fifty years. In either case the copyright runs until the end of the calendar year fifty years after the author's death.

Suppose you do not know if or when an author might have died. Does the copyright go on and on forever, sheltered by public ignorance? No; the law provides that if, seventy-five years after first publication of a work or one hundred years after its creation, the records of the Copyright Office contain no information as to the author's being alive or as to when the author died, the author will be presumed to have been dead for fifty years. Anyone who in good faith relies on this presumption may not be held liable as an infringer. The only requirement is that he must obtain from the Copyright Office a certified report that it has no information on the subject. Presumably he will be able to continue using the work even if he subsequently learns the author has not been dead for fifty years, although the statute is not explicit on this point.

Anyone who has a stake in the copyright can file a statement with the Copyright Office, indicating that the author is still alive, or that he died on such-and-such a date. This may or may not be desirable, of course; it would actually shorten the copyright term if the author dies fewer than twenty-five years after publication of his work or in some cases fewer than fifty years after its creation.

There are exceptions to the life-plus-fifty rule. Mask works receive only a ten-year term, measured from the date of registration or from first commercial exploitation, whichever occurs first.[29] The most important exception, however, is that for works made for hire. Copyright in a work made for hire lasts for seventy-five years from the data of first publication or one hundred years from the date of creation, whichever is the shorter period. Suppose, for example, that in 1978 a publisher of a children's story commissioned someone to illustrate it as a work for hire, and the story, complete with illustrations, was published in 1979. The writer has a copyright in the story for her lifetime plus fifty years, but copyright in the illustrations, which are made for hire, lasts for seventy-five years (that is, through December 31, 2054). However, if the book is not published until 2012, copyright in the illustrations would expire in 2079 (one hundred years from the date of creation) rather than in 2087 (seventy-five years from the data of publication). These provisions also apply to any joint work if any contribution to it is made for hire.[30] Thus if the story and illustrations I have just described were considered parts of a joint work, the work-for-hire duration rules would govern.

The term for a work that is authored anonymously or under a pseudonym is much the same as for a work made for hire. If the records of the Copyright Office contain no information as to the true identity of the author, the copyright term, like that of a work made for hire, will be seventy-five years from first publication or one hundred years from creation, whichever period expires first.

At any time up to the expiration of this period, anyone who has a stake in the copyright can file a statement in the Copyright Office revealing the identity of the author.[31] As of that moment the copyright term becomes life plus fifty years (unless of course the work is also a work made for hire). This may not be desirable; if the author died, say, five years after publishing the work, revealing the author's identity will actually cause the copyright term to be shorter than it would have been if he had remained incognito. This situation creates an opportunity for the unscrupulous. Suppose that a movie producer owns the movie rights to a novel written under a pseudonym and has made a film that still, fifty years after the author's death, continues to produce yearly revenues. A rival film company, by buying up some other right in the novel, could obtain a stake in the copyright and be entitled to file a statement revealing the author's identity. The work would then be in the public domain, and the rival would be able to make a film of its own.

There is no way to avoid this result. However, if you are publishing a work under a pseudonym, you should require in every contract by which you transfer any interest in your copyright that the purchaser promises not to reveal your identity unless doing so will lengthen your copyright term. You should also require every purchaser to make the same demand of everyone purchasing from him. In this way you will preserve a right to sue for damages if a statement is filed to your detriment.

3

Transfers of Copyright

An argument can be made that the word *property* refers not to possession of a thing but only to the right to use or dispose of it. It is this, I think, that underlies our use of the word *property* for so intangible a thing as copyright.

Because copyright is property, it can be sold, given away, donated to charity, bequeathed by will, or rented out on whatever terms the owner desires. And the same is true of any subsidiary right, such as the right to publish, the right to perform, and so on. However, copyright differs from most other kinds of property in two important respects:

First, the property of individual authors (as opposed to corporations that are authors of works made for hire) is immunized in an unusual way from government interference. Until an individual author has made at least one exclusive license or grant of his copyright, or some part of it—for example, the right to perform the work publicly—no part of his copyright can be expropriated, transferred, or confiscated from the author by any court or other governmental body for any purpose or any reason (including, presumably, nonpayment of taxes), except in the context of bankruptcy.[1]

Second, a sale or other transfer that appears to be absolute and irrevocable may be revoked (or "terminated," to use the language of the statute) by the author or by his heirs, provided that certain procedures are followed. This is a statutory right and does not affect any right of termination that the author may have reserved by contract.

Of these two special rules, the second is likely to be the most important in years to come. It was enacted to prevent a recurrence in the future of the sad tales we know so well, in which the hero signs away his copyright for a pittance only to see the villain reap enormous profits. Whether the new rule will have any practical value for the average work remains to be seen.

Making a Transfer

A transfer, often referred to as a grant, of a copyright or any right under it, can be either exclusive or nonexclusive, depending on the needs of those involved. Nonexclusive grants tend to be for limited periods of time; for example, a high school theater company needs no more than a nonexclusive license for its spring play. A book publisher, on the other hand, will insist on getting an exclusive publication right in a manuscript.

A nonexclusive license can be as informal as a handshake. It can be inferred from the conduct of those involved. But can it be imposed on someone who otherwise would be merely the buyer of a copy? That is the issue presented by the kind of "license" often used on over-the-counter software. This "shrink-wrap" license, so called because of the kind of plastic wrapping used on the diskette package, purports to change what would otherwise be the sale of an object into a license of copyright by saying, "By opening this package you will be indicating your consent to the following terms." The legal validity of this approach is open to doubt. A Louisiana statute that was enacted expressly to validate shrink-wrap licenses has been struck down, on the grounds that only Congress can legislate in this area.[2] But the underlying question of validity remains at large.

An exclusive license or other exclusive transfer—be it a mortgage, sale, gift, or bequest—must be in writing and must be signed by the person making it. With regard to unpublished works, this did not use to be so. The old rule was that common law copyrights could be transferred orally or even by implication.[3]

The only instance in which an exclusive transfer does not need a signed instrument is where it comes about by what is called "operation of law." For example, if an author dies without a will, the law of the state where she lives will give her copyright to her heirs, and no written instrument is needed.[4]

"Exclusive" is not so narrow as it seems. You can give an exclusive license to perform a play in Alaska if you put the agreement in writing and sign it. You can give an exclusive license to perform a play for a limited period of time, say, five years. You can give one person an exclusive license to distribute a work by mail and another person an exclusive license to sell over the counter.

Any limit on a license must be expressly stated.[5] If the license is in writing, the limitation should be as well; if the license is by word of mouth, the limitation must be clearly understood by both parties.

Sometimes, though, even written limitations on a license are less clear than they seem. For example, writers of stories or novels frequently give movie producers something called "motion picture rights." This phrase and others like it have created a lot of litigation over whether television broadcast of the movie is permitted by the license. (The source of the contention is that television is not the traditional means or place of showing a movie.)[6] The cases have gone both ways, depending on minor differences in wording. This and similar problems of interpretation underline the need for careful drafting of licenses. This particular problem can be avoided by a clause something like, "The producer will have the right to perform and display his motion picture in any manner and by any means now known or later developed."

The only clear exception to the rule that limitations on a license must be expressly stated is for contributions to collective works. Here the statute reverses the general rule. It provides that if you contribute, say, a poem to an anthology, the owner of the anthology can publish it only in that anthology, revisions of that anthology, or later works in the same series, unless you give a broader license. A contribution to a magazine would be another common example; the publisher is presumed to acquire only the right to publish it in issues of that magazine. This is a major departure from pre-1978 law.[7]

Can a license be transferred? In other words, can a licensee give someone else part or all of his license? Here too the law has changed since 1977. Under the old law sublicensing, as this is called, was not allowed unless the licensee was clearly given that right.[8] Under the new law the answer depends on whether the license is exclusive or nonexclusive. It is fairly clear under the new statute that an exclusive license can be transferred unless the copyright owner has specified otherwise.[9] However, nothing in the new law seems to have changed the old rule with respect to nonexclusive licenses.

Copyright Licenses Distinguished from Sales of Objects

As has been mentioned, copyright in a work exists separately from the tangible forms in which it may be fixed. Transferring ownership of a painting, therefore, does not transfer copyright in it. And the reverse is also true: transferring copyright does not give the new copyright owner any right to possess the actual painting or other work.

In this respect the law has changed, for it used to infer a transfer of copyright from transfers of the physical object, if the work were unpublished.[10] In essence the law assumed that if you were parting with the means of reproduction—be it a painting, photographic negative, in some cases even a manuscript—you intended to empower the new owner to reproduce the work. The abandonment of this old rule is one of the more dramatic pro-author shifts in the 1976 Copyright Act.

Transfer of the means of reproduction may possibly be evidence of a nonexclusive license, or of a waiver of rights by the creator, but that would be the extent of it.

Drafting a Transfer Agreement

The written instrument necessary for an exclusive transfer can come in many shapes and sizes, and may be executed at any time before or after the transfer takes effect.[11] A written memorandum of the transfer will suffice if it is signed by the transferor. A letter from an author to her mother describing the transfer could satisfy the requirement if a court found it to be adequate evidence. If you are getting a license and are afraid that someone will try to question the existence of the transfer—for example, by claiming that the author's signature is forged—have the instrument of transfer notarized.[12]

For the benefit of all concerned, any copyright transfer should clearly state, in addition to royalty provisions, warranties, and so on, the answers to the following questions:

1. What rights are being transferred? If the entire copyright is transferred, a clause often used is "*X* hereby transfers to *Y* his entire right, title, and interest, including copyright, in and to a certain work entitled *Mud Wrestling for Fun and Profit.*" Otherwise be quite specific; for example: "*X* hereby transfers to *Y* his entire right to perform publicly a certain work entitled *Mud Wrestling for Fun and Profit*"; or "*X* hereby licenses to *Y* the exclusive right to make audiovisual works based on *X*'s work entitled *Mud Wrestling for Fun and Profit.*"

2. How long is the transfer to last? What other limitations are there?

3. When, how, and for what reasons can the transfer be terminated? (If not at all, nothing needs to be said on this point.)

4. Whose name will be placed in the notice on any published copies? Every contract concerning publication should require that the person receiving the grant place proper copyright notice on all published copies. [13] (See chapter 4 for a fuller discussion of copyright notice.)

5. Who will bear the cost of prosecuting or defending any infringement suit?

6. How will damages won in any such suit be apportioned?

7. Who will pay if someone wins an infringement suit against the work?

To keep their dealings with their authors private, many publishers are limiting their instruments of transfer to a brief description of the transfer and dealing with the other issues (points 3 through 7) in a separate contract. Thus when they record with the Copyright Office, they file only a single sheet of paper. This is a practice I recommend to anyone drafting a copyright agreement. If you follow this practice, your separate contract should state, "The instrument of transfer concerning this work is incorporated in this contract by reference and made a part of this contract." In this way the two documents are tied together for other purposes.

Recording the Transfer

The written evidence of a transfer—be it a contract, a memorandum, or a letter—may be recorded in the Copyright Office. The fee is $10 for recordation of up to six pages concerning only one work; each additional work and each page over six will incur an additional $.50 to the fee. For example, recordation totaling eight pages and covering two works will be charged a fee of $11.50.[14]

When recordation has been completed in the Copyright Office, the person who records will receive a certificate of recordation; duplicate certificates can be obtained from the Copyright Office for $4 apiece.[15]

Recordation that clearly identifies the work will give general notice to the world at large of the facts set forth in the recorded document. Other people are presumed to have notice of all the information recorded, regardless of whether they have actually seen the document. For this is to be so, however, the work must also be registered (see chapter 5).[16] Recordation of a transfer cannot be used as a substitute for registration of the underlying work.

Two People Claiming the Same Right

One important effect of recording a transfer is to establish priority of ownership. Suppose that a novelist sells dramatization rights in his novel to Smith on April 1 and then on April 2 sells the same rights to Jones. Smith has a one-month "grace period" in which to record the transfer (two months if the transfer is executed outside the country). After that time it is a horse race: Jones will be regarded as the legal owner of the copyright if he records before Smith, even though the transfer to him took place later than that to Smith.[17]

But again this is true only if the work has been registered. Thus we see the lengths to which Congress has been willing to go to induce people to register copyright claims. If the work is not registered, or until it is registered, no one has priority over anyone else, and neither Smith nor Jones may sue the other for going about his business. It is therefore in the interest of anyone who is recording a transfer to ensure that the work is registered.

There are two important circumstances under which these rules of priority do not apply. First, if the later transfer is a gift or bequest it cannot take precedence over a sale that preceded it, no matter when the sale is actually recorded.[18] This result seems only fair; it would be hard to justify a law that gave precedence to someone who had paid nothing for a right over someone who had paid. Second, if the person who received the second transfer actually knew of the first transfer, he cannot take precedence over the earlier purchaser by beating him to the Copyright Office. This too seems only fair.

The question of priority occurs not only between one transfer and another but also between a transfer of ownership and a nonexclusive license. Suppose, for instance, that a playwright sells performing rights in her play to a Broadway producer and later in the week gives permission to a local troupe to perform the same play. If the nonexclusive license was taken by the local troupe without knowledge of the prior transfer and before the transfer was recorded, the troupe has the right to perform the work within the limits of its license without regard to the rights of the producer. This is so regardless of whether the nonexclusive license itself is in writing and regardless of whether it is recorded.[19]

Suppose in another instance that the nonexclusive license is given before the sale of rights is made. Here, again, the nonexclusive license takes priority over the transfer, regardless of whether or when either of them is recorded. The nonexclusive license in such a case is like a right-of-way over a piece of land: any purchaser of the land is obligated to honor the right-of-way.

In no instance does it matter whether the nonexclusive license was paid for or was a gift or bequest. In this the law with respect to nonexclusive licenses differs fundamentally from the law of exclusive transfers.

Recordation of Licenses for Public Broadcasting

If you give any public broadcasting station or network a license to perform or display a published musical work or to display a published work of art, whether or not you also give it the right to tape the performance or display, you should require it to record the license within thirty days. If the license is not recorded, you will be bound by the terms of a compulsory license created by statute (see chapter 7).

Termination of Transfers

In addition to any termination right an author may reserve in a contract, the author and his heirs have a termination right under the copyright statute. The statutory right of termination, unlike the copyright itself, cannot be contracted away, given away, or bequeathed. No agreement that anyone can persuade an author to sign will diminish his right or the right of his heirs to terminate a grant of copyright.[20] For this reason a contract clause requiring the author to pay the other party money if he exercises his termination right would probably be held invalid under the new law. In short, the right to terminate is not a property right but a privilege under the law. It extends to all works other than those made for hire and to all grants except those of rights in foreign countries.[21]

In general only grants made by a living author, and made after December 31, 1977, may be terminated. Other grants, even those made by the author in his will, are not subject to termination.[22] An exception for certain pre-1978 works is discussed in chapter 9.

After termination the person who once owned the right or license cannot exploit the work further in any way. There is one exception: if someone has made a derivative work under a grant permitting him to do so, he can continue to exploit this work, because the derivative work has a separate copyright. Termination prevents him only from making or authorizing further derivative works. Moreover, any royalty income from that derivative work will continue to be paid as it was before termination, even if this means that an intermediary, rather than the terminating author, receives the benefit.[23]

The statutory termination right is open only to authors, their widows or widowers, and their children and grandchildren (whether legitimate or not and whether natural or adopted). Someone else who has received a right from an author, or even the entire copyright, and transferred to a third person, has no termination right.[24]

The right is also limited in time. Termination may be made only in a five-year period beginning thirty-five years after the date of the grant and ending forty years after the date of the grant. The only variation from this rule is the case of a publication right. The five-year period in which a grant of a publication right may be terminated can begin at one of two times: either forty years after the date of the grant or thirty-five years after the date of first publication, whichever is earlier.[25]

Certain procedures must be followed in exercising this right. These procedures apply whether the original grant or license was exclusive or nonexclusive; even a word-of-mouth license cannot be terminated except by following the rules:[26]

If the work is a joint work, and two or more of the joint authors execute a grant, termination may be made only by a majority of those authors who executed the grant. The law does not require a majority of the interest in the work, only a numerical majority of the authors who made the grant. Because nonexclusive transfers of copyright in a joint work can be made by one joint author without the others' consent, the termination rules focus on who made the grant, not who owns the copyright. In other words, even if one of three joint authors is entitled, by agreement with the others, to 60 percent of the royalties, he cannot singlehandedly terminate a grant unless he alone made it. The majority requirement also means that if only two authors executed the grant, they must both join in the termination for it to be effective.

Just what obligations one joint author has to another in this respect is unclear. Co-owners are liable to each other for profits and, in many cases, for loss they may cause to the income-producing ability of what they own. Will joint authors be liable to each other for loss of revenues if the loss is caused by termination of a grant? My guess is that they will not be, because the termination is a legal right created by statute.

If an author or a joint author is dead, his right to terminate or to join in a termination may be exercised by his surviving spouse (regardless of remarriage) and his children or grandchildren. The spouse controls half of the right and the children or grandchildren the other half. If there are no children or grandchildren, then the spouse controls the entire right, and if there is no spouse, then the children and grandchildren control the entire right. The statute makes no provision for an author being survived only by great-grandchildren. It is not clear why great-grandchildren were given no rights under the statute, but that is the case.

If children or grandchildren own the termination right, or one-half of it, what they own is to be divided among them in equal shares. This division into shares is a *per stirpes* distribution. This means that if, for example, an author's daughter is dead, but has surviving children, her share belongs to her children and may be exercised only by a majority of them. If all of an author's children are dead, the surviving grandchildren do not take equally; each set of grandchildren takes the share that would belong to their parent if he or she were alive.

The required percentage: The termination right of a deceased author may be exercised only by persons owning, among them, over 50 percent of the termination right. For example, if there are a widow, one child, and three grandchildren of a deceased child, then the widow owns 50 percent of the right, the child owns 25 percent, and the three grandchildren among them own 25 percent, but can exercise their 25 percent only if a majority of them agree. In such a case termination can take place only if the child or two of the grandchildren agree to terminate. If there are a widower, one child, and two grandchildren, then either the child or both grandchildren must join with the widower. If there is no spouse, but there are three children, then two of the children must join together.

Notice of termination must be given in advance. This notice must be in writing and must be signed by the necessary persons or their authorized agents. It must specify the exact date on which termination is to become effective. That date must be within the appropriate five-year period. Notice itself must be given at least two years before that date, but not more than ten years before it. Notice must be recorded (for a $10 fee) in the Copyright Office before that date, or it will be invalid. The notice must be served, in person or by first-class mail, on "the grantee or the grantee's successor in title," that is, on the person who originally received the transfer, or on anyone who has obtained it from him.

This language is anything but self-explanatory. Suppose the grantee (the person who received the transfer) has sold it to someone else without your knowledge. If you serve notice only on the grantee, will that terminate the rights of the person he sold it to? If we say "yes," we are perhaps creating hardship for the second purchaser. If we say "no," we are perhaps creating hardship for you, the author.

Neither the statute nor the regulations of the Copyright Office shed much light on this problem. It will be one for the courts to clarify. My guess—or, more accurately, my hope—is that the terminator will be held only to his own personal knowledge of what subsequent transfers have been made and to a knowledge of any transfers recorded in the Copyright Office. If the author is a composer whose work is handled by ASCAP, BMI, or one of the other performing rights societies, he will also have a duty to check the society's records. If his search reveals no "successor in title," it will be enough that he has served notice on the original grantee. This puts the burden on the successors in title to record the instruments by which they obtain their rights, and that seems not only a fair allocation of the burden but one in keeping with the law's general policy of encouraging recordation.

Copyright after Termination

As of the date that notice of termination is served, the right or rights that are to terminate become vested in the persons who own the termination right.[27] For example, as of the date that a playwright's widow and children terminate his grant of the performance rights, the performance right vests in them. Vesting means entitlement, not actual possession; what happens is that the rights that will eventually revert, when the termination takes effect, are allocated before that time, and are a limited kind of property interest.

The rights vest in everyone who could have joined in the termination, regardless of whether he actually did take part in it. If, for example, an author's son did not take part in giving notice of termination, he will still get his proportionate share of the right when it reverts. If the termination is made by the family of a deceased author, the rights vest in the same *per stirpes* manner described previously. In the case of a joint work, nothing vests in an author (or the family of an author) who did not join in the original grant, because he did not own a termination right with respect to that grant.

Making a New Transfer

Because vesting is less than actual possession, the rule that the rights vest as of the date notice is received does not mean that the new owners can make a new transfer immediately. They cannot make a new grant of any kind, exclusive or nonexclusive, before the date of termination; not even the author can do this. Moreover, with one exception, those in whom the right vests cannot even make a commitment to make a grant before the date of termination. And because selling the right to make a grant is tantamount to making a grant, it is probable that even someone who receives the entire right, when that right vests, cannot sell his right to make a new grant until the date that termination takes effect.

The exception to this rule is that the people terminating may renegotiate a contract with the existing right holder.[28] For example, if a publisher has a license to make and sell reproductions of a photograph, the photographer or her appropriate heirs can give notice of termination and immediately thereafter renegotiate the contract. The renegotiated royalties do not, theoretically, take effect until the date that termination actually occurs, but if the license is lucrative, the publisher may well compromise on this point and pay more royalties in the interim to get a renewal of the grant.

It is important to remember that the right to terminate inheres in the person; it is less like property than like a privilege. It cannot be sold or given away. If an author's widow dies, the termination right that she possessed dies with her, and the entire termination right belongs to the children or grandchildren, if any. If they in turn die and leave no descendants of their own, the whole privilege comes to an end, and the license or transfer will continue on for the rest of the copyright term, immune from termination. However, once notice of termination is given and reversion of the copyright becomes vested in the people who had a right to terminate, we are talking not of a privilege but once again of a property right.

Unlike the right to terminate, this property right does not die with the owner; he can bequeath it in his will to anyone at all, and whoever receives the bequest can take part in any renegotiations or new grants. Presumably, also, the owner can sell or give away his right to receive income from his share of the copyright. But unless he owns the entire copyright, he cannot sell or give away during his life his right to take part in making a new grant because the law makes very stringent requirements for new grants of terminated rights.

Mechanics of Making a New Transfer

A renegotiation, or a new grant, must be made in the following manner.[29]

1. It must be in writing. This requirement applies not only to transfers but also to nonexclusive licenses. (This is the only circumstance in which a non-exclusive license is required to be in writing.)

2. It must be signed by persons representing at least the same proportion of ownership in the right as was involved in the termination.

3. It must be signed by the same number of persons as signed the notice of termination.

These requirements concerning number and proportion are difficult to grasp. It may be helpful to take an example. Suppose that an author dies, survived by a wife, one daughter, and two grandsons born of a deceased son. Because termination of the original grant requires participation of over 50 percent of the termination right, in this case it will require 75 percent of the right—the widow's 50 percent, plus another 25 percent from either the living daughter or the deceased son as represented by his children. It will also require at least two signatures.

When the right vests in the author's family, upon the giving of notice of termination, it vests 50 percent in the widow, 25 percent in the daughter, and 12½ percent in each of the two grandsons. (Each of these people now owns a separate and distinct interest because the rights are vested.) Suppose the widow then dies, bequeathing her entire share of the right to one of the grandsons, so that he now owns 62½ percent of the right. The law provides that someone who inherits an interest in a right in this way "represents" the person from whom he received it, for purposes of signing a new grant. Thus the grandson represents his grandmother, and he may sign the new grant on behalf of his grandmother as well as on his own behalf, so that in effect there are two signatures on the document. This meets the "number" requirement because there were only two signatures on the notice of termination. However, despite the fact that he now owns over half the right, the grandson cannot singlehandedly make a new grant, for the new grant must be agreed to by 75 percent of the ownership—that being the percentage of the ownership which agreed to the termination. Therefore, to make a new grant, this grandson must persuade either his brother or his aunt to join him. If he cannot, no new grant can be made.

Once a new grant or a renegotiation of an old grant has been made, it binds and benefits everyone who had a share of the right to make it, regardless of whether he actually signs the new grant or renegotiation.[30] In the previous example, if only the widow and the two grandsons join in making the new grant, the daughter is nonetheless treated as if she too had joined in. By "binds" I mean that when the new grant is made, she cannot make a grant of any kind on her own; on the other hand, she is entitled to her share of the proceeds. To take another example, if an author's husband and one of her two children terminate an old grant and then renegotiate it or make a new grant to someone else, the other child cannot go off on his own and arrange a separate sale, but on the other hand he is entitled to a 25 percent share of the profits that the rest of the family has negotiated.

4 Copyright Notice

Just as much as copyright is property, it is also a bundle of procedures, paperwork, and footwork. These need to be followed scrupulously to protect a copyright.

Common law copyright is acquired upon creation of a work and lost upon fixation of it in tangible form. For purposes of the federal statute, you acquire copyright upon fixation of the work, and at any point before completed fixation you automatically have copyright in as much of the work as you have fixed. Until the United States joined the Berne Convention, a multilateral copyright treaty, on March 1, 1989, another important rite of passage was "publication." Under our pre-Berne law, once a work was published, you forfeited copyright if you did not affix notice of copyright to it.

This is no longer so. Notice is not required for works published after March 1, 1989. Works published before that date, however, will continue to be governed by the pre-Berne rules. And even though notice is no longer required, it is still advisable, because it deprives an infringer of the defense of innocence.[1] So in applying the rules that follow here it is critical to determine first whether the work in question was published during the period from January

1, 1978 to February 28, 1989, or earlier, or later. If later, then the rules governing copyright notice are advisory only; if during, then they are mandatory. If earlier, then even more stringent rules apply in some respects, and these are discussed in chapter 9.

Publication

The concept of publication has been crucial to copyright law from the beginning. Publication is the act of offering copies to the public. There does not have to be an actual distribution.[2] Even if there is a distribution, it does not have to be a sale; giving copies away to the public is sufficient. The size of the public is irrelevant; handing out one or two copies can constitute publication.[3] And though performance or display of a work is not publication in and of itself, distributing copies to a group of persons who will themselves perform or display the work does count as publication, unless those persons are your employees or otherwise act under your control.[4]

The sale of one's painting, sculpture, or other work of visual art probably constitutes a publication in the eyes of the law, although there is some evidence that Congress did not intend this result.[5] But this is not a cause for great concern, because the rules of copyright notice do not require that a notice be placed on the original of an art work if no other copies are produced.

Performance and display of a work do not constitute publication. You can perform or display a work as often as you like, to as wide an audience as you like, and you will not be considered to have published it by doing so. (Both "performance" and "display" include broadcasting, film projection, and so on.)[6] Delivering a speech does not publish it.

Nor does circulation of copies within a limited group, for limited purposes, count as publication.

However, the persons receiving those copies must understand that they have no right to perform or display them publicly or to make a further distribution outside the group.[7] Nor is the filing of copies or phonorecords with a court or other public authority a publication.[8]

Submission of a manuscript to a publisher is a classic example of "limited publication," as it is called, for which copyright notice is not required and would indeed be inappropriate. In the academic community there is also a custom of circulating so-called preprints (manuscript copies of forthcoming journal articles) among colleagues for comment and discussion. This too would be a limited publication in most cases. But if you are making what you intend as a limited publication under circumstances where your intent will not be absolutely clear to your audience, you would be well advised to place on the copy either a regular copyright notice or a legend to this effect: "This copy is circulated for comment only and may not be used or distributed in any other manner."

A friend of mine in the profession once told me that at cocktail parties—those wonderful clearing houses of free legal advice—the question he is most often asked is, Who owns copyright in letters? Why does this question seem to trouble so many apparently respectable citizens? Whatever the reason, the answer will comfort them, for it is the writer who owns copyright unless there is some clear indication to the contrary. However, the recipient would have the right to make the letter public if it were necessary for some reason—perhaps to his defense against a libel action, or to clearing his character, or something of that sort.[9]

When Is Notice Required? In the case of copies from which a work can be "perceived visually," copyright notice should be placed on all copies publicly distributed, whether in the United States or elsewhere. It is not necessary that visual perception be possible with the naked eye; it is enough that the copy distributed can be perceived visually with the aid of a machine or device, such as a movie projector. Remember that musical works are regarded as being visually perceived when they are written in musical notation, and the same applies to notation of choreography.

Sound recordings are works that by definition cannot be perceived visually. They are not distributed in the form of "copies" but in the form of "phonorecords." The term *phonorecord* is a hybrid word adopted by the new law. It includes records, tapes, player-piano rolls, and any other method now known or discovered in the future for fixing sounds, but it does not include the soundtracks of audiovisual works.[10] Every phonorecord that is distributed to the public should bear notice of copyright with respect to the sound recording that it embodies. However, no notice of copyright in the underlying music or other work need be affixed to the phonorecord.

A new and interesting question, which no court has yet faced, concerns the computer programs that embody so-called computer music. These programs are written to drive the synthesizers that both imitate (or embellish) sounds of more traditional instruments and create entirely new sounds of their own. By the time they enter the synthesizers (which are computers connected to sound-producing mechanisms), they are in disk, tape, or other object code form. In such a tape or disk a phonorecord of a sound recording or a copy of a musical work? Like any more conventional phonorecord its primary function is to cause a machine to produce sound. On the other hand the program begins life as a series of written notations, which can be likened to ordinary musical notation, and hence constitutes a "copy." Under current doctrine an object code version of a source code program is a copy of it, not a derivative work. Thus, by an equally logical train of thought, we can conclude that the disk or tape is a copy of the musical work, not a phonorecord.

For now, this conundrum is merely intriguing. But the day is probably not far off when there will be a market for computer music among a large segment of the public who can afford to own synthesizers, and floppy disks of computer music will occupy a corner of every music store. Should they bear copyright notice as copies or as phonorecords? (For the moment you'd be wise to use both.) How should the source codes be registered—as musical works or as sound recordings? Will it be possible to acquire a compulsory license (see chapter 7) to make other floppy disks of the same music? If so, what will be the scope of the license? It seems that fewer problems will arise if we consider the disk to be a copy of the underlying musical notation, but I would hesitate to predict that this will in fact be the rule.

Notice for Contributions to a Collective Work

One question frequently asked is, What notice is needed on a magazine article, or a poem in an anthology, or any other contribution to a collective work? All contributions to a collective work are protected by a general notice affixed to the collective work as a whole, except for advertisements, which must bear separate notice.[11] However, under the pre-Berne rules, if the contributor retained copyright, omission of separate notice might be treated as if notice had been given in the wrong name. It was and still is a good idea to require, if you can, that your contribution to a collective work have its own copyright notice.

Formalities of Copyright Notice

Notice comprises three things:

1. In the case of visually perceived works, the familiar symbol © or, if you prefer, the word *Copyright* or its accepted abbreviation, *Copr.* (If you wish to be certain that your work is protected in foreign countries, use ©; *Copyright* and *Copr.* do not have international validity.) In the case of sound recordings published in phonorecords, the only symbol to use is Ⓟ; © is of no effect. In the case of mask works there are three options: the words *mask work*, the symbol *M*, or the symbol Ⓜ.[13]

2. The year of first publication. This date is not necessary for mask works or where a visual work is reproduced in or on greeting cards, postcards, stationery, jewelry, dolls, toys, or "useful articles" (articles having an intrinsic utilitarian function).[14] A good example of this useful-article exception would be the reproduction of a painting on a placemat; in such a case the date when the painting itself was first published would not need to be included in the copyright notice.

Bear in mind that the year of first publication of a work may not necessarily be the year in which you first need to affix copyright notice. For example, a musical work is considered to be "published" by the distribution of phonorecords or movie soundtracks embodying it, even though those phonorecords and soundtracks do not need to bear notice as to the musical work. Thus if a piece of music comes out on a record in 1984 but not in written form until 1986, 1984 is the proper year to put in the notice.

3. The name of the owner of copyright. This may

be abbreviated if the name remains recognizable. If the owner has a generally known trademark, abbreviation, or other symbol, that symbol may be used instead. This term *owner of copyright* is different from the term *copyright owner* (who may be merely the owner of the exclusive publication right). The owner of copyright is the author or anyone to whom the author has transferred the entire copyright or the bulk of copyright.[15] In the case of a sound recording, notice must be in the name of the owner of the copyright in the recording; the name of the owner of copyright in the musical composition should not be used and may lead to substantial confusion.

There is an additional requirement in the case of works that consist preponderantly of works of the U.S. Government. For example, a collection of public documents edited by a private citizen must include in the notice a statement identifying those parts of the work that are the author's and in which copyright is therefore claimed, or those parts that are the product of the U.S. Government and in which copyright is therefore not claimed.

The elements of notice need not appear all together, so long as they are all present on the copy and placed in such a way that a reasonable person would understand them to be parts of a whole.

The location of the notice as a whole is important, although the law's requirements have not, since 1978, been so strict as formerly. In the case of sound recordings, notice must be placed on the surface of the phonorecord, or on the label, or on the container in which the phonorecord is retailed. Its placement must be calculated to give "reasonable notice" to the public. In the case of visually perceived works, the only requirement is that placement be calculated to give reasonable notice to the public. Notice has to be fixed to the copy or phonorecord; the law will not be satisfied by, say, tying to a sculpture a tag with copyright notice written on it, unless no alternative is feasible. The regulations of the Copyright Office, giving examples of acceptable placement of notice, are reproduced in appendix A.

The principle that notice be "reasonable" has led to some judicial loosening of the rules. For example, it has been held that as long as notice appears on one of a group of items that are sold together, it will cover all those items. Thus it was sufficient to place notice on the cardboard box in which a toy puppy was sold, but not on the puppy itself, because the box was intended to be kept as a "kennel" for the puppy.[16]

As additional protection, it is advisable to place in your notice the statement "All Rights Reserved," to ensure protection in certain Latin American countries that do not recognize *Copyright, Copr.*, or © as proper notice of a claim of rights.

Incomplete or Omitted Notice

If any one of the three principal components of proper notice—name, date, and the symbol, word, or abbreviation for copyright—is omitted, the work will be treated as if notice were omitted entirely.[17] Where the work consists preponderantly of U.S. Government works, and the notice does not say so, the work will be treated as if notice were omitted entirely.[18]

Omission of notice, under the *ancien regime*, destroyed copyright, casting the work into the public domain. This was not true, however, in these cases:

• the omission was in violation of an express understanding between the copyright owner and whoever was responsible for publication, or

• the notice was omitted from only a relatively small

number of copies that were distributed to the public, or

• the application for registration, complete with fee and the necessary number of copies, was filed before the date of the publication from which the notice was omitted, or

• the complete application for registration was filed within five years after first publication, and a "reasonable effort" was made to add notice to all copies distributed to the public within the United States after the omission was discovered.

These "cure" provisions would still be available to works published before Berne accession, if the five-year period has not yet run.

A few comments on these exceptions are in order. No one knows what a "relatively small number of copies" was or is. Twenty thousand copies of a book with a printing of 100,000 is the same percentage as one bronze casting out of a limited edition of five, yet the latter would have been acceptable and the former probably not. "Relatively," in other words, had only the vaguest of meanings. This was another instance where the law would look to what was fair and just in a particular situation.[19]

Difficult problems may yet arise in cases involving works of fine art. A painting does not need to bear copyright notice when the painter sells it; a unique canvas comes with the exception we are discussing here. But a lithograph in an edition of 200 is a different story. If the artist omitted notice from, say, 40 copies published in 1986, fails to register his copyright, and fails to make a reasonable effort to correct the omission, and if a purchaser of one of the 40 copies relies on the absence of notice and starts reproducing the work himself, the artist might be out of luck. If the court decides that 40 is a relatively large number of copies in an edition of 200, the work will have entered the public domain—and copyright, once lost, can never be regained.

What was or is a reasonable effort to correct an omission? Here too, as with work for hire, we have a question for ad hoc determination on which the circuit courts have split doctrinally. In the Second Circuit one must make an attempt to affix notice to copies that have not yet been sold at retail, even if they are already in the hands of distributors or wholesalers. The other circuits that have ruled on this are more lenient.[20]

What happens to a copyright owner who has failed to stipulate in a license agreement that the licensee will be responsible for proper notice? If the licensee's effort to correct notice is later found not to have been reasonable, the copyright owner, though practically powerless to correct the fault, may have lost his copyright. Can he sue the licensee? That remains to be seen.

The total effect of these rules has been to make it virtually impossible at any given moment to know whether a work published during the years 1978 to 1988 without proper copyright notice is in the public domain or not. The matter is further complicated by the rule that forfeiture of copyright in a derivative work, such as a doll based on a cartoon, did not affect copyright in the original, as long as the forfeiture was not sanctioned by the copyright owner of the original.[21] This whole foggy state of affairs made it easier in the end for Congress to sweep away the notice requirement altogether.

Defective Notice

What happens if a notice is facially correct, but information contained in the notice is erroneous? Under pre-Berne law the consequences of erroneous notice could be serious if the copies or phonorecords bearing defective notice were distributed with the copyright owner's permission. Thus, anyone signing a contract with a publisher would have been wise to require the publisher to place correct notice on the copies or phonorecords. Otherwise a court might assume that the faulty publication was made with the author's consent. Defective notice on unauthorized copies or phonorecords—for example, albums distributed by a record pirate—or on copies or phonorecords distributed in violation of the terms of the contract did not affect the rights of the copyright owner at all.

On the other hand, pre-Berne law had a valid interest in making copyright owners responsible for seeing that copies or phonorecords distributed with their permission bore correct notice. The consequences of a mistake differed depending on the nature of the error. (I am referring to unwitting errors. Fraudulent misrepresentations in a copyright notice could, and still can, bring a fine of up to $2,500.[22])

Mistake in Name

If the person whose name appeared in the notice was not the real owner of copyright—for example, if a book bearing notice in the name of John Adams was actually the work of his wife Abigail, or if a publisher that had only the publication rights put its own name on the notice, or if a contribution to a collective work did not bear a separate copyright notice—the copyright notice retained some value; the public was put on notice that at least somebody claimed copyright in the work. What if someone in good faith purchased rights in the work from the person named in the notice and proceeded to exploit them? If the copies bearing erroneous notice were published before U.S. accession to Berne, the law states that the purchaser will be considered an innocent infringer if he "begins his undertaking" before the work has been registered in the correct name or before some other document has been recorded with the Copyright Office, signed by the person whose name appears in the notice but revealing the true owner of copyright.[23] This does not mean that the good-faith purchaser actually gets a right in the work; he does not. What he gets is a sort of limited privilege to exploit the right he believed he was buying. This will likely remain true post-Berne.

Fairness requires such a result. If the law were otherwise, many unlucky purchasers would find themselves with no way to recoup their investment. Because fairness is the guiding principle, however, no one can say in advance how a court will decide a particular case.

Pre-Berne law provided that this limited privilege not exist until the purchaser "begins his undertaking." Clearly these words mean more than the mere act of purchasing the right because at that stage the whole problem could be corrected simply by undoing the sale. Only an investment of time and resources in actually exploiting the right will tip the scales in the purchaser's favor. Will setting type be enough? Will hiring extra personnel be enough? As to that, no one knows, for this provision of the law has not been tested. Perhaps now it never will be.

And what is the extent of the limited privilege that the purchaser thus obtains? If, for example, he has sunk money into a big Broadway production in reliance on his bogus right, he will probably be permitted to exploit his bogus right at least until he has recovered his investment, perhaps even until he has made a reasonable profit. After that, does his privilege end? Again the law is silent.

From the perspective of the copyright owner

whose rights are infringed, the situation is no less fraught with ambiguity. The law provides that he is entitled to receive the profits of the person who sold the bogus right. Suppose the seller has inadvertently sold the rights for a fraction of their true worth? Can the true owner sue anybody for the difference? Probably, but no one knows for certain.

Mistake in Date

If the date written in the notice was earlier than the true date of first publication, in the ordinary case there were no repercussions. But if the work were published anonymously or under a pseudonym or were a work made for hire, so that the copyright term would be computed with reference to the first date of publication, the term would be computed from the date given in the notice, and the copyright owner would lose a year or more of protection.

If the date given in the notice was later than the date of first publication by only a year, there were no repercussions. However, in the case of a work published anonymously or under a pseudonym or in the case of a work made for hire, the date given in the notice will be ignored, and the copyright term will be computed using the correct date.

If the date in the notice were two or more years later than the actual date of first publication, then the pre-Berne statute treated the work as if the date had been omitted altogether.[24]

These rules apply only to erroneous notice on copies published before U.S. accession to Berne on March 1, 1989.

The Innocent Infringer

In drafting the 1976 act, as Congress wrestled with the need to loosen notice requirements, it also wrestled with the plight of the unwitting infringer. Suppose somebody, seeing no copyright notice, decided the work was free to all? To protect this honest wretch proved to be, however, no simple task. In its final form the 1976 act exempted him from liability only if he was "misled" by the absence of notice. If he had reason to believe the work actually was copyrighted, was he under a duty to investigate? If a work that is obviously original lacks copyright notice, the first instinct of any moderately sophisticated person would be to suspect that this omission was an error. Could one who has such a suspicion still be "misled"?

Although this unauthorized user was, technically speaking, infringing the copyright, Congress decided to protect him from some of the penalties of infringement. For example, until it was actually brought to his notice that the work was registered with the Copyright Office, he could continue to publish without fear of liability for damages. He might or might not be required to surrender his profits; that would rest with the discretion of the judge or jury hearing the case. Furthermore this infringer might or might not be required by the court to stop publication or, if permitted to continue, might or might not be required to pay royalties to the copyright owner. Under no circumstances would he be required to compensate the copyright owner for damages. Damages in this context would include injury to an artist's reputation due to the circulation of poor copies of his work; they would also, presumably, include whatever harm might result from the fact that the copies or phonorecords distributed by the infringer bore, themselves, no copyright notice. In light of these problems it is clear that registration, which put such users on notice of the copyright claim, was an important safety measure.

The innocent infringer is still with us. The elaborate notice rules I have described continue to apply where copies or phonorecords were published before the U.S. accession to Berne, even if the lawsuit is heard now. Post-Berne is another story. We know that there is still an innocent-infringer defense, but who can invoke it is not entirely clear. The statute can be read to say that if notice is defective in any degree, no matter how slight, "innocence" may be found. It is unlikely, though, that this is how the statute will be interpreted. More likely the 1978–1988 notice rules will continue to apply, only instead of having the power to throw a work into the public domain, they will measure the rights of the copyright owner against a *particular* infringer who saw a *particular* copy of the work. One thing we can say for certain: it is as wise now as it ever was to put proper notice on every published copy of a work.

Notice On Confidential Materials

One question often asked by people in business is, What sort of copyright notice does one place on materials that contain trade secrets—know-how, customer lists, business methods, and so on? It is not an easy question to answer. Now that the law regarding notice has changed, there seems less reason for concern on this point. But for those asserting trade secret rights, a bare copyright notice has never seemed particularly helpful. It does not warn users against the actions that most worry the owner of the materials.

My suggestion is to place a legend to the following effect on copies distributed on a confidential basis:

The within material is an unpublished copyrighted work containing trade secret and other proprietary information of XYZ Corporation. This copy has been provided on the basis of strict confidentiality and on the express understanding that it may not be repro-

5

Registration of a Copyright Claim

Registration does not affect the existence or validity of a copyright. It is, however, important as a method of protecting one's rights under the copyright, for these reasons:

1. It can be of crucial importance if for any reason notice of copyright is accidentally omitted from copies of the work that are distributed to the public.

2. It is in many cases a prerequisite for bringing suit to enforce a copyright. (If you have attempted to register in the proper manner, but the Copyright Office has rejected your application for any reason, you may still file suit for infringement, but you must give the Copyright Office notice of your suit.[1])

3. You cannot get an award of attorneys' fees or of so-called statutory damages for any infringement that takes place before the "effective date" of registration. (The effective date of registration is the date on which the application, fee, and deposit were filed, regardless of when they were finally processed.) Registration, in other words, creates the right to receive these special compensations. In the case of a published work, there is a three-month grace period for registration. If you apply for registration within three months of first publication, you can collect attorneys'

fees and statutory damages for any infringement that takes place after publication. However, there is no three-month grace period for unpublished works except works first fixed when broadcast.[2]

4. If you are the owner of copyright in a musical work, you are not entitled to royalties under a so-called compulsory license until your identity is a matter of record with the Copyright Office. In practical terms this makes registration a prerequisite to receipt of those royalties. There is no three-month grace period here.

Who May Register

Anyone who owns or has an exclusive license for any of the rights comprised in the copyright of the work may register the work. It is the work that is being registered, not any of the subsidiary rights that make up the copyright. Registration is of the basic underlying claim in the original work.

Who Must Register In Order to Sue?

Before Berne accession every copyright owner wishing to sue an infringer had to register his copyright as a prerequisite to suit. If he were not the author of the work, he also had to record with the Copyright Office the instrument by which he acquired rights in the work. These requirements were incompatible with Berne, which permits no formalities as a prerequisite to copyright protection.

Under the new law the latter requirement, recordation of transfers, has been scrapped altogether, and the registration requirement has been limited so as not to apply to works whose country of origin is a member of Berne other than the United States. The registration requirement still applies to U.S. works and to works from foreign countries that do not belong to Berne. It also applies to mask works regardless of origin.[3] It should be noted, though, that registration and recordation may still be required for suits on infringement that occurred before March 1, 1989.[4]

Determining the "country of origin" is more complicated than the words might suggest. A work is exempt from registration if it passes one of three tests, which I shall call the author test, the country of publication test, and the location test.[5]

The Author
Test

If at least one of the authors is a citizen of a Berne Convention country other than the United States or is domiciled in such a country, or has his or her "habitual residence" there, the registration requirement is waived. In the case of a published work, this test is applied as of the date of first publication. In the case of an unpublished work, this test appears to be applied as of the date the suit is brought, although that is unfortunately less than entirely clear. (The alternative would be to apply the test as of the date of creation of the work.) A special rule applies to audiovisual works: if the work is an audiovisual work, any corporation, limited partnership, or other "legal entity" that is the author is considered to be a "national" of a foreign Berne country only if it has its headquarters there, regardless of where it is officially incorporated.[6]

The Country of
Publication Test

Even if it fails the author test, a work will avoid the registration requirement if it was first published in a Berne country other than the United States. However, if the work is first published simultaneously in a foreign Berne country and in the United States— for example, simultaneously in Canada and the United States—the work will be treated as published abroad, and thus exempt from registration, only if the foreign country's law grants it a shorter term of protection than does U.S. law. For example, in some Berne countries photographs, sound recordings, works of industrial art, computer software, and mask works are protected for much shorter periods than in the United States. These works, if published simultaneously in those countries and in the United States, will be exempt from registration. Publication is "simultaneous" in two countries if no more than thirty days elapse between the two publication dates. Note that simultaneous first publication in a *non*-Berne country does not affect the outcome of this test.

The Location Test

A pictorial, graphic, or sculptural work will be exempt from registration if it is "incorporated" in a building or structure located in a Berne country other than the United States. This would include, for example, murals and ornamental works that are embedded in the fabric of buildings; it would probably also include (although the language is ill chosen for this result) architectural plans that are embodied in buildings. Thus, for example, if an American builder photocopied the plans of an Italian building, the Italian architect would not have to register in order to sue.

Overall, though at the cost of almost jesuitic intricacy, these rules achieve the goal of encouraging registration for works of U.S. origin. If you ask "Why?" or "So what?" you would not be alone. And yet the Library of Congress depends in large measure on the registration system for the thoroughness of its collections. Moreover, in a country as large as the United States, with such a vast and diverse output of copyrightable works—larger and more diverse than in any other country in the world—it is a benefit to have as complete a public record as possible.

**How Is
Registration
Accomplished?**

An application for registration has three components: the registration form, the filing fee, and deposit of copies of the work.

The Form

The registration form used will vary depending on
the type of work being registered. For a nondramatic
literary work other than a periodical or serial work,
use form TX; for a periodical or serial work, use form
SE; for a dramatic work or any other work of the performing arts (including music, dance, and film,
among others), use form PA, unless you also own
copyright in the sound recording of the work and are
simultaneously registering your sound recording
copyright, in which case you should use form SR; for
a work of the visual arts (not including film or other
audiovisual works), use form VA; for a sound recording, use form SR. For a computer program or database use form TX, unless the audiovisual displays are
the predominant part of the work, as they might be
in a video game. In such a case use form PA. These
forms do not vary much in content, but each requests
information that is especially important to the type of
work it covers. These forms are available from the Information and Publications Section, Copyright Office, Library of Congress, Washington, D.C. 20559, or
can be ordered by telephone at (202)287-9100.

All of the forms require certain basic information:[7]

1. The name and address of the copyright claimant.
An owner of any subsidiary right under the copyright is not a "copyright claimant"; that term is used
only for the author or for someone who has acquired
the basic, underlying claim from the author by sale,
gift, or inheritance.

2. The name of the author(s), unless the work is
published anonymously or under a pseudonym.

3. The nationality or domicile of the author(s),

even if the work is published anonymously or under a pseudonym.

4. If one or more of the authors is dead, the dates of their deaths.

5. If the copyright claimant is someone other than the author(s), a brief statement of how the claimant came by the copyright.

6. If the work is a compilation, a statement identifying the preexisting work or works that it incorporates; if it is a derivative work, a statement identifying the work or works on which it is based. These statements should also identify in a general way what material is original with the claimant, because that is all that is covered by the claimant's copyright.

7. A statement that the work was made for hire, if it was so.

8. The title of the work and, if in its finished state it had any other titles by which it might be identified, those other titles as well. This is particularly important if the work has been published before under a different title, a not infrequent occurrence in the case of books that were first published outside the country. The word *identified* refers to identification by the public; you need not include titles by which the work has been known only to the author or private viewers. In general if the work you are registering contains material that appeared in a different form under a different title, you would be well advised to make note of this fact when registering.

9. The year in which "creation of the work was completed"—that is, the year in which it was fixed in its final form, disregarding minor editorial changes. Remember that different versions of the work, if they differ substantially, are considered to be separate and distinct works; you should mention previous ver-

sions of this type not under this heading but in the space where you are asked if the work is a derivative work.

10. If the work has been published, the date of its first publication and the nation in which that first publication took place.

In any of these categories do not omit any information that may bear on the validity of the copyright claim. If you do so unintentionally, you may suffer much in lost time and money. If you do so intentionally, you run the risk of being fined up to $2,500.[8]

To illustrate how a registration form should be filled out, I have included a sample completed form TX as appendix B.

The Fee

The application form must be accompanied by a $10 fee, unless the registration is of a claim for a renewal of a copyright in a work published before January 1, 1978, as to which see chapter 9.[9]

Deposit

The application must be accompanied by deposit of either one or two copies of the work or, in special cases, some other kind of material that will identify the work you are registering.

The rules governing deposit are quite complicated. First of all, although deposit is always made with the Copyright Office, it is intended not only for the purpose of registration but also for the archival purposes of the Library of Congress.[10] A single deposit can satisfy both of these requirements, but for it to do so, it must be made at the same time that the registration application is filed or be accompanied by a letter asking the Copyright Office to hold it until the registration application is filed.[11] If deposit is not made under one of these two circumstances, the Copyright Office will forward it to the Library of Congress, and you will have to make a separate deposit when you register your copyright.

Deposit with the Library of Congress can be required even if you have no desire or intention to register your copyright. If the Librarian of Congress decides that the Library should have a copy or copies of your work, the Register of Copyrights will send you a written demand for deposit. You have three months to comply; if you do not, you will be liable for a fine of $250 and for any expenses incurred by the Library of Congress in acquiring copies of your work. If your failure to comply is willful or repeated, you may also be liable for an additional fine of $2,500.[12]

The following rules govern deposit with the Library of Congress:[13]

1. Only published works will be held by the Library. Unpublished works may have to be deposited for registration purposes, but not for purposes of the Library of Congress unless by some special arrangement between the author and the Library.

2. The following types of published works are exempt from deposit with the Library:

• Scientific or technical diagrams and models. Architectural plans, blueprints, and models are covered by this exemption.

• Greeting cards, picture postcards, and stationery.

• Lectures, sermons, speeches, and addresses unless they are published in an anthology or collection. Anthologies and collections are not exempt from deposit, even if all the contents are the work of one person.

• Literary, dramatic, or musical works on which phonorecords are based, unless those works are also published. In other words if a sound recording is made of a piece of music, for example, but the music itself is never published in print form, the fact that the sound recording is published in the form of phonorecords does not subject the underlying musical work to the deposit requirement.

• Sculptural works.

• Works embodied only in useful articles or in jewelry, dolls, toys, games, or plaques. For example, if a design is published only by being printed on textiles, it is exempt from deposit for the Library of Congress. Maps and globes are not defined as useful articles and do not come within this exemption.

• Advertising material, including labels.

• Tests and answer material for tests, if published separately from other literary works.

• Works that were first published as contributions to collective works. The collective works themselves are not exempt, only the individual contributions.

• Musical or other works that are published only in movie soundtrack form. This exemption is very similar to that concerning literary, dramatic, or musical works published only in phonorecord form. It means that if a musical work, for example, is not published except in a movie soundtrack, no separate deposit requirement applies to it.

• Television programs whose only publication has been by virtue of a license granted to a nonprofit organization, permitting the organization to make videotapes of it.

3. For published works that are covered by one of these exemptions, the general rule is that you must deposit two copies of the "best edition." (The current standards for determining what is the "best edition" are reprinted in appendix C.) However, there are certain kinds of works for which a single copy of the best edition will suffice:

• Two-dimensional visual works, so long as no more

than four copies of the work have been published, or, if more than four copies have been, the publication has been in the form of a limited edition of no more than three hundred, of which every copy is numbered. If your work qualifies for this special one-copy arrangement, you can also satisfy the deposit requirements by depositing photographs or "other identifying material" instead.

• Motion pictures but not other audiovisual works. Also with regard to motion pictures it is possible to enter into a "Motion Picture Agreement" with the Library, permitting you to ask for immediate return of your deposit copy on the stipulation that the Library may demand it back at any time in the following two years.

• Globes, relief maps, and other three-dimensional cartographic works.

• Musical works published only by rental, lease, or lending but not by sale.

• Multimedia instructional kits. Multimedia for these purposes means anything involving literary works, audiovisual works, and sound recordings, or any combination of two of these types.

4. Works published in the form of holograms are covered by special rules. In addition to two copies, you must deposit two sets of precise instructions for displaying the image and two sets of photographs or other material that will identify the image.

5. If you are depositing copies of a phonorecord, you must deposit with it any label or package on or in which it is usually sold.

6. The Register of Copyrights, in conjunction with the Library of Congress, can grant special absolution from the deposit requirement if you can give persuasive reasons why your work should be exempted. If you wish for such treatment, you must submit your

request (and your reasons) in writing to the Chief of the Acquisitions and Processing Division of the Copyright Office. Any request must be signed by either the owner of the underlying copyright or the owner of the publication right. Thus the owner of only the performance right in a work right cannot apply on his own to have the work exempted from any deposit requirements.

7. If you would like a receipt for your deposit, you can obtain one by paying a $2 fee.

The rules governing deposit for registration purposes are slightly different. For one thing there are no exemptions; and deposit may be a prerequisite for registration. There are differences in the deposit requirements between one type of work and another, and some of these differences are similar to those in the Library of Congress context, but you should be very careful not to confuse deposit for registration with deposit for the Library.

The rules for registration deposit are as follows:[14]

1. Only one copy is required to register an unpublished work. (A motion picture is not considered to be published merely because a nonprofit institution has been given a license to make a fixation of it. For example, if a school is given permission to videotape a television broadcast, the television program is still unpublished for deposit purposes though not for other purposes.)

2. As with Library of Congress deposit, the basic rule for published works is that you must submit two copies of the best edition. However, one copy of the best edition will suffice for these types of published works:

• Two-dimensional visual works, as long as no more than four copies have been published or, if more than four have been published, as long as publication has been in the form of an edition limited to 300 or fewer, all copies being numbered. Any visual work qualifying for this one-copy arrangement can also be deposited in the form of photographs or other identifying material.

• Motion pictures but not other audiovisual works.

• Globes, relief maps, and other three-dimensional cartographic works.

• Scientific or technical diagrams. Architectural plans and blueprints come under this exception.

• Greeting cards, picture postcards, and stationery.

• Lectures, sermons, and similar material published individually and not as part of a collective work.

• Contributions to a collective work. The deposit for registration of a contribution to a collective work should be of a copy of the collective work as a whole.

• Music published only in notational form or, if in phonorecords, only by rental, leasing, or lending.

• Multimedia instructional lists.

• Advertising materials, including labels. If one of these was published in a magazine or other periodical, it is sufficient to deposit just the page of the periodical on which it appeared, not the entire periodical. If a print or label is physically inseparable from a three-dimensional object—for example, if it is stamped on the base of the object—different rules apply. (See point 4.)

• Tests and answer material for tests, if published separately from other literary works.

• Designs that are published only by being printed on textiles, wallpaper, wrapping paper, and similar merchandise. If the design is repeated on the material, the swatch submitted for deposit must show at least one repetition. However, if the only way that the design is published is by the incorporation of the textiles (or what-have-you) in dresses, furniture, or

other three-dimensional articles, different rules apply. (See point 4.)
• Works first published abroad. In such a case the one copy deposited should be a copy of that first foreign edition, not a copy of the best edition.

3. You can make deposit in the form of identifying material rather than in the form of a copy or copies for certain kinds of works:
• Unpublished two-dimensional visual works.
• Published two-dimensional visual works, as long as no more than four copies have been published or, if more than four, as long as publication has been in the form of an edition limited to 300 or fewer, all copies being numbered.
• Unpublished motion pictures (but not other kinds of audiovisual works).
• Unpublished works fixed only in motion picture soundtracks.
• Works that are published only in the form of motion picture soundtracks.

4. For certain kinds of works, the only proper deposit for registration purposes is in the form of "identifying material":
• Sculptural works, models, and maquettes.
• Computer programs and databases (see appendix D for a fuller discussion).
• Unpublished visual works that are fixed only in useful articles, or in jewelry, toys, dolls, or games.
• Published visual works, if they are published only in useful articles or in jewelry, toys, dolls or games. This category includes visual works that are published only by virtue of the fact that the textile or other material on which they are printed is used in making a three-dimensional article. For example, if a design is printed on fabric used to upholster chairs, and the only manner by which the design is pub-

lished is the sale of chairs upholstered in that material, then deposit must be made in the form of identifying material. Neither this category nor the previous one includes visual works that are embodied in useful articles that are part of a multimedia educational or instructional kit.

• Works for which the copy deposited would be larger than eight feet in length, width, or height.

• Advertising material that is physically inseparable from a three-dimensional article. For example, if the design of a label is stamped into the base of a lamp, to copyright the label design, you must make deposit in the form of identifying material.

5. There is a special additional requirement for motion pictures, whether published or unpublished. If you deposit in the form of a copy or copies, you must also submit a synopsis or some other description of the contents of the motion picture.

6. There are also special benefits given to motion pictures. First, the Library of Congress is given thirty days from the effective date of registration (the date on which registration, deposit, and fee are received) to decide whether it wishes to keep the copy or copies that have been deposited for registration. If it does not make a decision within thirty days or if it decides it does not want the motion picture for its archives, the copy or copies will be returned to the applicant. Second, as an alternative to this you can enter into a Motion Picture Agreement such as I have described. Third, the Copyright Office will accept motion picture soundtracks as deposits for purposes of registering simultaneously all works contained in them, including music.

7. There is a special additional requirement for holograms. For each copy submitted, you must also

submit precise instructions for displaying the image and some kind of material clearly showing the image.

8. The Register of Copyrights can permit you to deposit one copy instead of two, or to deposit an incomplete copy or copies, if you can present a convincing reason why you should receive special treatment. A request for special treatment must be signed by the applicant. (This signature rule is less strict than that for the Library of Congress deposit.) To make such a request, write to the Chief of the Examining Division of the Copyright Office. This is a different person from the person to whom you submit such requests in the Library of Congress context. You can combine the two requests; if you do so, the Chief of the Examining Division is the person to address, and the application must be signed either by the owner of the underlying copyright or by the owner of the publication right.

The identifying material that can be used to satisfy the deposit requirement is a photograph, transparency, drawing, photocopy, or any other two-dimensional reproduction or rendering of the work. For example, a photograph of a limited-edition woodcut or a drawing of a sculptural work will suffice. There are a few special rules:[15]

• Material reproducing two-dimensional visual works must reproduce the actual colors of the work. This is not true of material reproducing sculptural works.

• If you submit more than two pieces of material for any one work, all must be the same size.

• Transparencies must be 35 mm and must normally be mounted in cardboard, plastic, or similar materials. All other types of material must be not less than 3 × 3 in. and not more than 9 × 12 in.; the preferred maximum size is 8 × 10 in.

• Except in the case of transparencies, the image must be at least life-size, except that it can be less than life-size if it is at least four inches in any one dimension.

• At least one piece of identifying material must indicate the title of the work and the exact measurement of at least one of the true dimensions of the work.

• These rules do not apply to unpublished motion pictures or to works that are fixed or published only in the form of a motion picture soundtrack. For unpublished motion pictures, identifying material is composed of a description of the movie, together with either a phonorecord of some kind, reproducing the entire soundtrack, or a set of visual reproductions of single frames—at least one frame from each ten minutes of footage. The description may be a synopsis, a continuity, or anything of that sort, but it must include the title and also the episode title, if it is an episode; the nature and general content; the date of first fixation; the date of first transmission; if the work was fixed simultaneously with transmission, a statement to that effect; the running time; and the credits appearing on the work.

• Because copyright notice is no longer legally required, deposit materials no longer need to show notice. However, if you are prudent enough to use notice anyway, the identifying material you deposit should show where the notice is placed.

Multiple Registration

Because of the $10 filing fee, it would in many cases be a burden to the author to have to register separately every work he has created. Fortunately an exemption from the rigors of registration has been given to individual authors (but not joint authors) who contribute to periodicals.[16] An individual author may now register on a single form (form GR/CP), for a single fee, all works published in periodicals (including newspapers) in a given twelve-month period, provided that

1. Each of the works, on the occasion of its first publication, bore a separate copyright notice (separate, that is, from the general copyright notice on the periodical), and each notice identified the author in the same manner (for example, not by name in one issue and by pseudonym in another).

2. You attach one copy of each periodical (or, in the case of a newspaper, one copy of the relevant section of each newspaper) to your application.

3. You identify each work on your application form and state the name and date of the periodical issue in which it first appeared. (Slightly different rules apply if the registration is for renewal of copyright in contributions to periodicals published before January 1, 1978.)

Group registration such as this requires filing two forms: form VA, PA, or TX, depending on the type of work that your contributions happen to be, and form GR/CP. The VA, PA, or TX will contain all information except the titles of the works and the statistics of their publication; these facts will be put on the GR/CP.

Can You Register More Than Once?

It is possible under certain circumstances that you may wish to make a second registration of a work. In fact in the case of a work that you first registered when it was still unpublished, you will be well advised to register again when you publish it if you have changed the title. You will also want to make a second registration if the first registration was not made in the name of the true copyright claimant, or if the original registration was for some other reason unauthorized or legally invalid—for example, if it was made by someone not entitled to make it. However, these are the only circumstances in which the same version of a work may be registered more than once.

Correcting an Erroneous or Incomplete Registration

After you have registered, you may wish to correct certain information contained in your registration or to supply additional information. This may be done by filing form CA, the application for supplementary registration, along with a $10 fee. No additional deposit need be made. Supplementary registration does not change the legal validity of the original registration. Because of this, supplementary registration may not be used for adding to a list of works covered by a previously filed group registration. It may not be used to record transfers of copyright ownership. Nor is it an appropriate way to notify the Copyright Office of changes in the content of your work. If the content has changed so much as to constitute a new version, you should make a new registration, and if it has not, your old registration remains valid. Nor is it the right procedure to use if the original registration was made in the name of someone who was not the proper copyright claimant; in such a case a new registration must be made. Minor errors in the name of the copyright claimant, however, can and should be corrected by supplementary registration. Also form CA is sometimes used as a way of getting on the Copyright Office's index the titles of stories, songs, or other works that have been registered already but as parts of a collective work.

An application for supplementary registration may be made by the author, by anyone who has become a copyright claimant by dint of having received the underlying claim from the author, by the owner of any subsidiary right in the work, or by an authorized agent of any of these.

Reproduction of Works for the Blind and Handicapped

Space 8 on form TX (for nondramatic literary works) deals with reproduction of your work "for the use of blind or physically handicapped persons." Completing this part of the form is purely voluntary. By completing it you give the Library of Congress a special nonexclusive license to reproduce your work for the benefit of the blind and the handicapped. This reproduction may be in braille, in phonorecords that are specially designed for use by the blind and the handicapped, or in both media; the choice is up to you.

The terms of this nonexclusive license are as follows:[17]

1. It can be granted only for works that have already been published.

2. It can be granted only by a person who owns the exclusive publication right or the exclusive right to make a sound recording of a work.

3. The Library of Congress assumes the burden of ensuring that every copy or phonorecord carries proper copyright notice.

4. The license, being nonexclusive, does not prevent you, as the owner of the publication or sound recording right, from making other nonexclusive licenses of your right. You can even make an exclusive license or an absolute sale of your right subsequent to this, but whoever takes that exclusive license takes it subject to the special Library of Congress license.

5. The license will last for the duration of the copyright, unless it is terminated before that.

6. Termination can be made at any time, unlike termination of other nonexclusive licenses. You must give the Library of Congress at least ninety days' notice. To terminate, send a signed statement to the Li-

brary of Congress's Division for the Blind and Physically Handicapped. Once termination goes into effect, the Library cannot make any more copies or phonorecords, but it can continue to use the ones it has already made.

7. Someone who purchases an exclusive publication or sound recording right subject to this license can terminate the license in the same way.

8. After termination the license can be given again by filing a form CA for supplementary registration.

Certificate of Registration

When the Register of Copyrights approves your application for registration or for supplementary registration, the Copyright Office will issue you a certificate of registration or a certificate of supplementary registration. The certificate has no separate legal significance, but it is useful to have it in your possession in case the official record of your registration is misplaced by the Copyright Office. Moreover, in subsequent transfers and other contracts involving the copyright, it will prove convenient to refer to the certificate because it contains, or should contain, the exact description of the copyright. It will also inform you of the registration number, to which you should refer when making or terminating transfers of copyright. (The registration number will be changed if a supplementary registration is made.) Additional copies of the certificate can be obtained from the Copyright Office for $4 each.

6

Rights in
Copyrighted Works

One of the many respects in which copyright resembles property in land is divisibility. If you own a parcel of land, you can sell mineral rights to A, water rights to B, and a right of way to C, and still be considered the owner of the underlying property. Copyright too can be exploited in many different ways. It comprises five basic rights, which, along with certain limitations and exceptions, are set forth in the statute.

The Right to Copy

The right to copy is the right to reproduce the work in copies or phonorecords. With regard to sound recordings, this right is limited. Someone else is free to make a recording that blatantly imitates yours; only if he actually lifts sounds from your recording is he infringing. This rule shows practical wisdom. Two renditions of a symphony are bound to sound alike; it would stifle artistic competition to require performers to differentiate themselves in unproductive ways.

The statute also limits to some degree the exclusivity of the right to copy computer programs. It provides that anyone who is an "owner" of a copy of a computer program may make an object code copy of it, so as to be able to use it in a computer. Such a copy may not, however, be transferred unless the original copy is also transferred and unless the owner is also transferring whatever rights he may have in the program. The owner is also permitted to make copies for archival purposes, so long as the archival copies are destroyed if continued possession of the program "should cease to be rightful."[1]

Curiously the statute does not in so many words require destruction of the object code version when possession of the program ceases to be rightful, but one can only presume that this was an oversight and that any cessation of rights in the program would cover all copies made, as well as copies originally received.

It is not clear why these provisions were added to the statute at all. It is hard to believe that the concept of fair use, which I discuss in chapter 8, would not permit anyone in rightful possession of a program to take whatever steps might be necessary to make full use of it. Even more obscure, and more troubling, is the limitation of these statutory rights to the "owner" of a copy of a program and the apparent exclusion of a lessee. Did Congress intend to say, by negative implication, that inputting a program would not be permissible for a lessee without specific authorization? One assumes not, though the legislative history is ambiguous. As originally proposed by CONTU, this provision of the statute spoke of "possessors," not owners. Somehow, somewhere, the word was changed, and there is no public record as to why.

As I have mentioned, the law regards an object code version of a computer program as a copy of the program, not a derivative work. There seems no reason not to apply this to data bases as well. For example, inputting an English-language directory into a computer data base would be copying it, not "translating" it into a new language. In fact the same rationale would apply to the making of a computer-readable version of any work. Thus no one who makes a computer-readable version of any public domain work would have any copyright in it, unless some new elements are added. On the other hand, translating a computer program from one computer language to another *would* create a derivative work—assuming of course that anything survived the process other than the ideas or algorithms of the original.

The Right to Create Derivative Works

The general concept of "derivative works" has already been discussed. As with the right to copy, this right has also been limited by statute where computer programs are concerned. The "owner" of a copy of a program is entitled to adapt it to his own needs, but may not transfer the adaptation except with the consent of the copyright owner in the original. Again it seems unnecessary to have provided this in the statute, since the concept of fair use is surely broad enough to protect this kind of activity. Also, the limitation of the statute to "owners" ought not to be read as depriving lessees of a similar right.

As for sound recordings, the only derivative work that is covered by copyright is a rearrangement of the actual sounds of the recording.

It is possible to make a derivative work of a derivative work, but, as I have mentioned, anyone doing this should take great care to obtain all necessary permissions. If, for example, a company wishes to make dolls based on a movie character, it must buy the right to do so not only from the person who owns the movie rights but also, if the character in the movie was based on a novel or a cartoon, from the novelist or cartoonist as well.

The Right to Distribute Copies or Phonorecords to the Public

This is the right to publish and needs no elaboration. It should be noted, though, that once you part with a particular copy of a work you lose control over its further distribution. The buyer can sell it, rent it, throw it away, or whatever he pleases.[2] The only exception to this "first sale" doctrine applies to recordings of musical works; the owner of a cassette, compact disc, or other recording is not free to rent it to others. This exception was enacted in 1984, after intensive lobbying by the recording industry.[3] Attempts to enact similar exceptions for videos and computer software have so far failed, however.

The Right to Perform the Work Publicly

"Publicly" in this case means outside the normal circle of family and social acquaintances. "Perform" includes both live performance and indirect performance by means of electronic broadcasting and similar processes. In the case of a movie or other audiovisual work, to perform the work means to show it by means of a projector or other device.

The right to perform a work includes performance using phonorecords. However, the owner of a copyright in the sound recording does not possess this right of performance; it belongs to the author of the underlying work.[4] For example, if you have written a song and a singer has made a compact disc of it, you are the person who controls the playing of the CD in public; the singer has no voice in the matter. She cannot prevent the performance of her recording and receives no royalties from it. Of course you can sell the performance right to the singer if you wish, but the two rights are separate.

What, then, of a videotape, which in theory seems indistinguishable from a sound recording? Alas there is no logical consistency here. If you permit someone to make a videotape of a play you have written, that person, not you, controls public performance of the videotape. There is no logical reason for applying this principle to audiovisual derivative works and not to sound recordings. The causes of the inconsistency are more powerful than logic, though; they have their roots in history. The rule is like certain rules of grammar that you can only memorize and should not struggle to understand.

The law permits certain types of performances in spite of copyright. These exceptions are elaborately defined.[5]

An exception is created for performances by non-profit educational institutions in the course of face-to-face teaching activities. A performance in a Berlitz classroom, for example, would infringe the copyright because Berlitz schools are commercial, not non-profit. This exception does not apply to performance of audiovisual works if the person performing the work knows, or has reason to know, that the copy being used is an unlawful copy. Thus, for example, a teacher cannot show a film that she suspects was pirated.

Does this mean that a copy lawfully made, under "fair use" principles (see chapter 8 for a discussion of fair use), can be used in a classroom? For example, if our teacher has videotaped a television broadcast of a nature film with her VCR at home, may she show the videotape in class? The answer is certainly "no," even though the videotape itself was lawful. The Supreme Court decision that gave its blessing to home videotaping made clear that the activity was lawful provided the purpose was for "time-shifting," that is, home viewing at a time different from air time.

Another exception to the performance right is created by law for the use of radios or television sets in public places, provided that the equipment is the standard type normally found in private homes and that no separate charge is made to the audience. A common example is the television in your neighborhood saloon; if the customers are not charged for the privilege of watching, and if the television is an ordinary kind (not one with a five-by-five-foot screen), the bartender is not regarded as "performing" any of the broadcast works.

A related exception covers the cable systems used by hotels and apartment houses, which connect all of the rooms or apartments to a common antenna. Cable systems used by governmental bodies or nonprofit institutions are also exempted, so long as they are not used for any sort of commercial advantage, charge no more than enough to meet expenses, and are available either to anyone who wants to hook into the system or only to private viewers or listeners.[6]

Other exceptions are created by law for performances of nondramatic literary or musical works. The first is for educational broadcasts. It covers broadcasts whether on the air or by cable, so long as they are a regular part of the educational program of a nonprofit educational institution or a governmental body. A broadcast must be made primarily for reception in classrooms or "similar places normally devoted to instruction" (which, for handicapped persons, may mean their own homes) or on governmental premises. Interestingly, the school or governmental body making any such broadcast is free to make up to thirty copies of the program, so long as all except one archival copy are destroyed within seven years.[7] Just what can be done with the copies is unclear, but it seems fair to say that any educational use within the institution or agency would be all right.

A performance of such a work not for commercial

profit is also outside the scope of copyright. However, for a performance to fit under this exception, there must be no admission charge—or the profits must go to charity—and no compensation may be paid to any performer, producer, or promoter. Both of these conditions must be met: a free concert will be a copyright infringement if the performer receives any payment beyond reimbursement of expenses.

The privilege given to charitable benefit performances has one other important qualification. It is still possible for the owner of the exclusive performance right in a work to prevent such a performance, if he gives written notice of objection to the promoters or other persons responsible at least a week in advance.[8] The notice must comply with two rules.

First, it must be signed by the copyright owner or by the performance right owner, or by someone empowered to act on behalf of one of them, and the signature must be dated and accompanied by the name, address, and telephone number of the signer, printed legibly or typed. The notice must include this information:

1. Reference to the statutory authority on which you rely. The statute should be cited. It is 17 U.S.C. §110(4).

2. The date and place of the performance that you object to or, if you do not know this information exactly, as much information as you do know about it, as well as your source, unless your source is confidential.

3. The reasons for your objection.

4. Clear identification, by title and at least one author, of the work you do not want performed or, if you prefer, a blanket identification of a group of works that have something in common, which can be as general as being written by the same author or

published by the same publisher. If you choose the blanket-notice route, you must give the name, address, and telephone number of at least two persons from whom the other party can obtain a more specific identification of the works. Also, if your notice does not identify the copyright owner or owners of all the works, you must offer to provide that information, including names and last known addresses.

5. A statement that the persons will be free to go ahead with the performance if no admission charge is made and if no profit inures to the performers or the promoters, but that otherwise those persons may be liable for copyright infringement.

Second, the notice must be received at least a week before the performance. You can instead give brief notice by telegram, if you get a signed letter with all the above information to the proper party before the performance.

Exceptions for performances of nondramatic literary or musical works have also been made where the performance takes place as part of a service of religious worship or at a function organized and promoted by a nonprofit veterans' organization or fraternal organization. The latter exception applies only if the general public is not invited to the performance and if the organization uses any proceeds (after paying reasonable production costs) exclusively for charitable purposes. It is designed, in short, to permit the local VFW or Elks or what have you to hold a fundraiser for their members without paying royalties. It does not, by the way, extend to college fraternities or sororities unless the performance is held to raise money for charitable purposes that are specified in advance.

In addition the law has carved out some more specialized exceptions. A dramatic musical work (such as opera or a ballet) may be performed in a religious service. A nondramatic musical work may be performed in a store for purposes of advertising sheet music or phonorecords. And a nondramatic literary work may be broadcast to blind, deaf, or other handicapped persons by a governmental body, a public broadcasting station, a cable system, or a radio subcarrier. Either of the first two can make up to ten copies of the program and keep them on hand for this purpose or lend them to similar organizations for the same purpose.[9]

The only exception created for performances of dramatic literary works, such as plays, is in the case of performances for the benefit of people who cannot read normally. Such a performance may not be made for profit, may be made only once by any one group of performers or under the aegis of any one organization, and may be made only of works that were first published at least ten years previously.

Lastly, if a governmental or nonprofit body sponsors an agricultural or horticultural fair, it will not be liable for unauthorized performance of music at that fair unless it arranges for or is in charge of the performance.

The Right to Display the Work Publicly

Display, like performance, includes broadcasting and other mechanical forms of communication. Where audiovisual works are concerned, display should not be confused with performance: you perform a film by playing it in the usual way; you display a film by projecting isolated frames.

The display right is a significant change from prior law and is of great importance to artists working in the visual arts. Someone who buys a painting has the right to place the work on exhibit in a museum or to display it to the public in any other way, so long as the public are physically present at the place of display. But the buyer has no right, unless he specifically buys the right from the artist, to broadcast an image of the painting or permit anyone else to broadcast it. Moreover this limited right to display a painting is given only to buyers; people who rent, borrow, or lease works of art have no right to display them in any way outside the circle of their friends and guests.

When it created the display right, Congress was thinking of works of visual art. However, the most important (that is, economically important) displays now occur in the computer field. When a central database such as Dialog permits a subscriber to bring data onto a remote terminal screen, it is "displaying" the contents of the database. Some databases of course contain visual works such as scientific drawings—and, who knows, perhaps when the technology of screen picture resolution becomes good enough someone will put the contents of all the world's museums at our fingertips. If so, the ownership of display rights in paintings and other works of art will become economically significant.

Like the performance right, the right to control display of a work does not extend to display in the course of face-to-face nonprofit or governmental teaching. (However, as with performance, this does not give a teacher the right to display a copy of an audiovisual work if he knows or has reason to believe that the copy was unlawfully made.) Nor does the right to control display extend to display by a hotel proprietor or someone of that sort if all he uses to display the work is an ordinary television set and if he charges nothing to the public for the privilege of seeing the display.[10]

Exceptions are also made for display in a service of religious worship[11] and display, in an advertisement or a news report, of a useful work—for example, a pillowcase or a placemat—that lawfully incorporates a work of visual art.[12] Thus if a painter licenses a wildlife painting to a maker of plastic placemats, the maker can advertise the placemats without infringing the painter's display right.

Other Rights in Visual Works

In many European countries, and especially in France, the law has long protected artists even beyond the sale of their works, by what are known as the *droit de suite* and *droit moral*. *Droit de suite* is the right to share in the profits of future sales of a work; when a work is sold by one collector to another, the artist gets a portion of the profit made by the seller. *Droit moral* ("moral right") is the right to control alterations of the work, the right to prevent its destruction, and the right to be acknowledged as its author if one chooses (or when appropriate to disclaim authorship), sometimes referred to as the "right of paternity."

The Berne Convention requires all its signatories to give some measure of recognition to the moral right. At the time of U.S. accession to Berne, it was argued, by those who did not wish to rock the boat, that U.S. laws prohibiting false designation of origin of goods in commerce already, in effect, protected the right of paternity. This may have been wishful thinking.

Apart from federal law, nine states—California, Connecticut, Louisiana, Maine, Massachusetts, New Jersey, New York, Pennsylvania, and Rhode Island— have now enacted moral right statutes for works of fine art other than motion pictures and works commissioned for commercial purposes.[13] Connecticut prohibits intentional alteration or defacement of a work of fine art, and gives an artist the right to claim (but, curiously, not to disclaim) authorship. Maine,

New Jersey, New York, and Rhode Island prohibit the display or publication of a work with attribution to the artist, if the work has been "altered, defaced, mutilated, or modified" without the artist's approval. The artist is also given a right to be recognized as the author of his or her works, or even, for good cause, to disclaim authorship and have any attribution removed. California, Louisiana, Massachusetts, and Pennsylvania go further: they give the artist a cause of action against the owner of a work who alters or defaces it and prohibit destruction of the work without the artist's consent. Louisiana and Pennsylvania go so far as to declare that negligent conservation and grossly negligent maintenance are actionable by the artist.

California alone has also enacted a *droit de suite* statute, giving artists certain percentages on resales of their works.[14] It remains to be seen whether this statute will, as some curmudgeons have predicted, merely drive the California art market into neighboring states.

In time the moral right, if not the *droit de suite,* will probably become the law in this country. Certain members of Congress are avid supporters of the moral right and tried to incorporate it into the Berne accession bill. They were thwarted by the magazine lobby, which understandably feared any limit on an editor's power to rewrite a story or crop a photo. Exceptions can and probably will be carved out of the moral right, though, to protect such interests. The moral right can coexist peacefully with the copyright law; however, artists should be aware of one pitfall: If an artist has granted away all copyright interests in a work, the grantee will be entitled under copyright law to make derivative works based on it. This apparent conflict between moral right and copyright can perhaps be resolved by limiting the moral right's coverage to those copies that the artist himself has produced, leaving the copyright owner free to make new copies in which the original work is altered. (The artist may still have the right to remove her name from the attribution.) It will probably also be wise to deny the moral right to works commissioned for commercial purposes, as has been done in those states and most foreign countries that have moral right statutes.

So far as the right to prevent destruction is concerned, we should be wary of certain excesses to which the law has run in France. At least one artist in France has prevented the demolition of a building because his mural happened to be there enshrined. (The state statutes I have mentioned generally make specific exception for works incorporated in buildings.) We should also take care, if we do adopt this doctrine, that owners of works of art be liable only for willful destruction and not be burdened with an affirmative duty to preserve works that they purchase. In this respect the laws of Louisiana and Pennsylvania are a model to avoid.

Mask Works   In the area of rights as in other areas, semiconductor chip masks are subject to special limitations. The copyright owner of a mask has the exclusive right to reproduce the work by optical, electronic, or other means, and to distribute chips in which the mask work is embodied. The other rights generally afforded copyright owners are denied. Like most other copyright owners the owner of a mask work loses control of the distribution of chips once they are sold.

The Compulsory Licenses

Implicit in the ownership of property is the privilege of determining who reaps the profits of it and what those profits will be. This is true of copyright no less than of other kinds of property. But in recent decades our laws have tended to make exceptions to this privilege; in the case of copyright these are the so-called compulsory licenses.

The Phonorecord License

The first of the four compulsory licenses affects the right to make and distribute phonorecords of nondramatic musical compositions. In essence, once phonorecords of a piece of music have been distributed to the public in the United States (and remember that a movie soundtrack is not a phonorecord), any other person may make another sound recording of the work and distribute phonorecords of the recording.[1] Moreover, and more important, the artist who records the work under a compulsory license may arrange the music, though not the accompanying words, to suit his own style or interpretation, if he does not change the basic melody or what the statute calls, with admirable complacency, the "fundamental character" of the work. What "fundamental character" means, no one knows. Most probably this will be decided on a case-by-case basis.

To obtain a compulsory license, one must serve notice by registered or certified mail on whoever owns the underlying copyright in the musical work. If there are two or more owners, only one needs to be served.[2] If the records of the Copyright Office do not identify the copyright owner or do not give an address, or if the last known address yields no results, notice may be served instead on the Copyright Office. If the person seeking the compulsory license does not serve notice one way or another before distributing any phonorecords or within thirty days after he makes his first phonorecord, he cannot obtain a compulsory license, and his phonorecords will be copyright infringements.

At the top the notice should bear the caption, "Notice of Intention to Obtain a Compulsory License for Making and Distributing Phonorecords." It should state the title of the work and the names of the author or authors, so far as they are known. It should contain the following information about the person or entity seeking the license:[3]

1. The full legal name. All trade names and stage names used in the record business should also be listed, even if they are not going to be used in connection with this particular work. For example, if Bridget Mahoney, known to the world as Wanda Waverly, intends to take out the license, she should list both her names.

2. The full and complete business address used in the record business. A post office box number or similar address is not sufficient unless there is no street address.

3. A statement of the type of business organization used in connection with the record business—for example, individual proprietorship, partnership, corporation, or charitable foundation. Publicly traded

companies must identify themselves as such; other corporations must list their directors and officers and the names of every stockholder owning 25 percent or more of their stock. (The true beneficial owner is what is wanted here; if the stock is held by a trustee for someone else's benefit, the beneficiary's name must be given.) Every noncorporate organization must list the names of every true owner (beneficial owner) of 25 percent or more of the enterprise, and if any of these is an organization, it has to be identified in the same way as for actual licensees. Suppose that a private individual forms a joint venture with a corporation to make records. The joint venture is the licensee, but the corporation's officers, directors, and so forth must still be listed.

4. The accounting year. For example, if a company seeking the license keeps its books and pays its taxes on a June 30 fiscal year, that must be stated.

5. Every type of phonorecord that the licensee will publish, such as cassette, compact disc, or album.

6. The intended date of publication.

7. The name of the principal recording artist or group that is or will be involved.

8. The catalog number or numbers that published phonorecords will bear.

The notice has to be signed, and the name of the person signing has to be legibly printed.

If you are the copyright owner in the musical work, you will not receive any royalties under the compulsory license until the copyright has been registered and any other documents necessary to identify you have been recorded. However, these filings are not onerous, and they are all you need to do to receive a compulsory license royalty.

The amount of the royalty to be paid on each phonorecord distributed under a compulsory license stood in 1989 at either $.05 for each separate work on the phonorecord or $.01 per minute of playing time for each separate work, whichever might be larger. Effective January 1, 1990, and every two years thereafter, these rates ratchet upward to keep pace with inflation. Royalties must be paid every month, on or before the twentieth day of the month. Once a year every person making phonorecords under a compulsory license must send to the copyright owner an accounting statement showing his calculations of how many phonorecords he has distributed and any other relevant information. Failure to pay royalties on a monthly basis and to file accounts when they are due can result in loss of the license.

It is important to remember that royalties are to be paid to the copyright owner. This is the person who owns the sound recording right in the musical work, for that is the right that is being sublicensed to others. In almost all cases this will be the composer or someone who has obtained the basic copyright from the composer.

There are several qualifications to the compulsory license:

1. It may be obtained only if the primary purpose of producing phonorecords under it is to distribute them to the public for private use. Phonorecords made primarily for broadcasting or for background music systems cannot be made under a compulsory license. They must be expressly authorized by the copyright owner. However, sale of a phonorecord to a broadcaster, if the phonorecord is available to the general public, would not invalidate the compulsory license.

2. It may be obtained only if the original phonorecords were distributed with the permission of the owner of the underlying copyright in the music. In

other words, if a phonorecord of a musical composition is made without the consent of the copyright-owner, the distribution of such a phonorecord, being an infringement, does not give rise to a compulsory license in anyone else.

3. The compulsory license does not permit a subsequent producer simply to duplicate a recording made by someone else.

4. Every sound recording made under a compulsory license is copyrightable as a derivative work. But an arrangement of the music, made to suit the style or interpretation of a particular performer, will not be deemed a derivative work and cannot be copyrighted.

5. The compulsory license may be lost if royalties are not paid on time and if the required monthly and yearly statements of account are not sent to the copyright owner on time. In the case of such a default, the copyright owner may give written notice to the licensee, and if the matter is not remedied within thirty days, the license will terminate. If the license terminates, continuing to make or distribute phonorecords will be regarded as infringement of the copyright.

I should add that many performers do not go through the complexities of obtaining a compulsory license but instead deal directly with the copyright owner or with the Harry Fox Agency, Inc., a large phonorecord license clearinghouse located in New York City. "Harry Fox licenses," as they are called, are sometimes cheaper than the statutory license and are generally considered safer for someone who wishes to adapt music to his or her own style.

The Jukebox License

Until the new law went into effect on January 1, 1978, the performance of a nondramatic musical work by means of a jukebox was not considered an infringement of the performing right in the work unless the place where the jukebox was located charged an admission fee. The 1976 Act has ended this unconscionable state of affairs.[4]

Because the Berne Convention does not permit compulsory licenses for jukeboxes, the new revision of the law recasts the compulsory license royalty as a sort of floor to which royalties will sink unless music copyright owners and jukebox owners can negotiate an alternative. Negotiations will almost certainly supersede the compulsory license. Because these are the business of only a handful of industry groups on either side, I will not discuss the matter further here.

The Cable Broadcasting License

The third of the compulsory licenses involves performance or display of works by cable television and cable radio. The creation of this compulsory license does not take away from copyright owners anything they had before. On the contrary it is a long-awaited recognition of their rights. The Supreme Court had held in 1968 that cable transmissions were not "performances" and therefore not infringements of copyright;[5] the new law rectifies this anomaly and provides a new source of revenue for copyright owners in musical works, films, and other broadcast material.

The new statute has clarified the law governing cable television and radio in many ways and has drawn clear lines among cable transmissions that need not obtain a license, those that can acquire a compulsory license, and those that cannot obtain a compulsory license and are, by definition, infringements (unless specifically authorized).[6]

A cable transmission is an infringement of the performance or display right in a work if any change is made in the program containing the work, or if any change is made in the advertisements that immediately precede or follow the program or are interspersed in the program. The reason that such alterations constitute infringement is that a cable system that indulges in them is really playing the role of broadcaster, not simply of transmitter, and also is interfering with the justifiable expectations of advertisers. This rule is not absolute; alteration of advertisements is permitted for the purposes of advertising market research, if the research company doing the alteration has obtained the agreement of the advertiser, the broadcaster, and the cable system itself. Also there are certain circumstances under which the Federal Communications Commission permits or even requires alterations of the content of the signals. These exceptions, however, are of minor importance.

Cable transmission will also infringe copyright if it is not "simultaneous," that is, if it is recorded and then transmitted at a later time. The only exception is in the case of cable transmissions made in Alaska, Hawaii, or any U.S. possession or protectorate, and this exception is available only if the videotape copy made by the cable system is performed only once and is not changed in any way, and only if the cable system takes steps to ensure that no duplicate is made of its videotape. (The owner or other officers of the cable system must file a public affidavit that those steps have been taken.)

Cable transmission will also infringe copyright if it is not made available to the general public. Unless required by the FCC, any transmission that is made to a limited group, such as a group of pay-television customers, will infringe copyright unless authorized by the owner of the performance or display right. By this rule Muzak and similar systems are infringers if they transmit without specific authorization.

Those are the circumstances under which a cable transmission runs the risk of being regarded as an infringer. Unless one of these violations occurs, cable transmission of a *network-made* program is not regarded as an infringement, and no license of any kind is required for it.

The new compulsory license fee is levied only on the transmission of *nonnetwork* programs. Although there is no basis in logic for this distinction, it is true that network broadcasting revenues and the royalties that networks pay to copyright owners are structured to reflect the existence of cable transmission, and it is also true that cable extends into very few areas that are not served by one or another affiliate of each major network. Congress decided under these circumstances to leave network broadcasting where it found it. Even within the area of cabling of nonnetwork programs, Congress has made a further limitation: the cable system need pay royalties only for transmissions outside the area served by the broadcaster of the program.

The computation of royalties to be paid by cable systems is extraordinarily complicated. Payment of the royalties, like payment of jukebox royalties, is made to the Copyright Office, but the Copyright Royalty Tribunal is responsible for distribution. If you have reason to believe that a work in which you own the performance or display right is being transmitted by cable system, you must file a claim to that effect with the Copyright Royalty Tribunal during July of any given year. Partly because the computation of royalties is so complicated, the establishment of a claim to part of them will not be easy. If you believe that you are entitled to royalties, you will be well advised to hire a lawyer to present your claim to the Tribunal.

How will you know whether you have a valid claim? Every cable system is required to file a special statement with the Copyright Office twice a year, listing all the broadcasting stations whose broadcasts it has transmitted during the previous six months. This at least will alert you to the possibility that the particular program in which you have an interest has been cabled. Beyond this you are left more or less to your own devices.

Who is entitled to present the claim? The answer to this question depends on who owns the broadcast performance right in the work or the broadcast display right. If an author has written a play, for example, and sold or licensed to someone an exclusive right to perform that play by means of broadcasting media, the performer is the person who has the right to present a claim, not the author. If on the other hand the license is nonexclusive, the author is the person entitled.

In the realm of visual works, the same rule applies. If you, the artist, have given a television station an exclusive right to display our work by means of broadcasting, the station has the copyright that counts. On the other hand, if you have given the station only a nonexclusive license, you are the one who should present a claim to the Tribunal.

These rules determine who can present a claim for compulsory license royalties. The rules as to who can sue for infringement are different and more open ended. If an author has sold or licensed his performance or display rights in return for royalties, he can sue the infringer himself, because the infringement affects his income interest. A broadcaster, even one who has only a nonexclusive license, can sue.

Furthermore if the cable system has altered the content of a cabled program, the statute gives every broadcaster in the area where the cable system operates the right to sue, regardless of whether the broadcaster has any interest whatsoever in the particular copyright being infringed.[7]

In the case of a lawsuit, notice must be given to all persons whose interests in the copyright might be affected. This is indeed the general rule for all copyright suits.

The Public Broadcasting License

This license is for the benefit of PBS, National Public Radio, and other noncommercial broadcasters. It is a fairly narrow license, permitting only the performance of published nondramatic musical works and the display of published works of art.[8] It also permits a public broadcasting station or network to tape a show where the performance or display occurs and reuse the tape. It is not, however, a license to dramatize a musical work or to make any other kind of derivative work; nor does it extend to display of any compilation of works of art.

The license will supersede any privately negotiated license not recorded with the Copyright Office within thirty days of execution.

Every public broadcaster is required to keep cue sheets and other records concerning its uses under the license, and you as a copyright owner have the right to see them. You are not obliged to take any affirmative steps; the broadcaster will forward your royalties to you. However, if you do not register your copyright, the broadcaster may not know where to find you and after three years will not be obliged to pay you.

The royalty rates are established by the Copyright Royalty Tribunal. The current rates will be in effect through 1991, and will rise slightly in 1992. The entire public broadcasting license will expire at the end of 1992, unless extended by Congress.[9]

The Satellite Transmission License

The past decade has seen a proliferation of satellite dishes in people's backyards—and front yards too, for that matter. In rural areas these dishes often seem as big as the houses and cabins they serve. Where cable cannot economically reach, these dishes provide television viewers their only link to the airwaves.

To ensure dish owners access to national programming, in 1988 Congress enacted a new compulsory license. In fact, the license helps these viewers only indirectly: the direct beneficiaries are companies that retransmit television signals by satellite.[10]

The license is complicated, and to parse it thoroughly here would be inconsiderate to the reader. The salient points are these:

• For a satellite company retransmitting broadcasts of "superstations," the license applies not only to transmissions directly to home satellite dishes but also to transmissions to intermediary carriers such as local cable companies that capture the signal and deliver it to households.

• For a satellite company that wishes to retransmit network broadcasts, the license applies only where viewers cannot receive network broadcasts directly and do not subscribe to cable.

• As with royalties for the compulsory cable television license, royalties from the satellite license are held in escrow by the Copyright Office and divided up by the Copyright Royalty Tribunal.

• The fees are fixed by statute until the end of 1992, at which point new fees will be established by good faith negotiations or, if that fails, by compulsory arbitration.

• The license is due to expire at the end of 1994. Thus it may be viewed as an experiment, the results of which (political as well as economic) Congress will assess during the final year.

The license cannot be interpreted as giving any kind of encouragement to unauthorized decoding of encrypted satellite broadcasts. In fact, in the same act of Congress the penalties for unauthorized decoding are raised, and the penalties for selling decoding devices are raised by an order of magnitude.

8

Infringement and Fair Use

If copyright is like property in land, infringement is like moving onto someone's land without permission, chopping down trees, mining coal, and stealing water from the well. But unlike boundaries in land, the boundaries of a copyright are never clearly defined and frequently are not known until the end of a lawsuit. I can give, then, only general guidelines for determining those boundaries ahead of time.

Some cases are relatively easy. If an artist claims that someone has performed or displayed his work or made and sold copies of it without his permission, he has raised a simple question of fact. Either the defendant did these vile deeds or he did not. The difficult infringement cases are those in which the artist claims that someone else's creation is so like his or her own that it infringes the underlying copyright in his or her work.

In the early days of copyright law, the only theft for which the law took retribution was theft of the exact words of a writing. However, as the literary marketplace grew and new forms of literature emerged, and as the public began to pay more attention to the artist and the demands of the artistic ego, this literalism became untenable.[1] In the past few decades it is doubtful if even five infringement suits out of one hundred have charged the defendant with actually using the plaintiff's language, word for word. Suits now are more likely to allege theft of plot, theft of characters, theft of musical theme, and so on. Necessarily in such cases the courts make judgments that are at least partly intuitive.

How Does a Court Find Infringement?

The following are some of the factors that a court will consider when someone claims copyright infringement: *Did the defendant see or otherwise have knowledge of the plaintiff's work?* If not, the defendant will not be regarded as an infringer. This is the effect of the doctrine of subjective originality, which I have discussed above. Knowledge of a prior work, however, does not have to be conscious; the plaintiff will win if he can prove that the defendant must have been exposed to the work, even though the defendant may honestly have forgotten the event entirely.

Is the plaintiff's work original? This question is closely similar to the previous one, only we are asking now whether the plaintiff himself has a valid copyright on which to sue. If the elements he claims are infringed are things that in fact he took from someone else's work, whether knowingly or not, his copyright claim in those elements is invalid.

Is the copied material expression that can be protected, or is it only the author's ideas, or historical fact, or the like? Like the first two questions, this is a threshold test that, if determined adversely to the plaintiff, will be fatal to his case. As stated previously, in cases having to do with computer programs courts have been struggling for workable rules in applying this test, so far with mixed results.

Is the copied material merely a variation on an old theme, or is it the product of the author's invention? (This question is asked, for example, when the suit charges theft of story line.) If it is merely a variation, how closely do the defendant's details track the plaintiff's? Are the details unusual, or are they the sort that anyone would be likely to choose who set out to write a variation on the same old theme? One famous copyright judge has suggested, in the context of the sort of analysis described here, that upon any work "a great number of patterns of increasing generality will fit equally well" and that at some level of generality one should excuse similarity between two works.[2]

A related question is, *Is the similarity between the works dictated by their subject matter?* Remember that where there are only a limited number of ways of expressing an idea, the "merger" doctrine denies copyright to any of them.

Details can be misleading, and to avoid this danger courts will frequently step back some distance and ask, What is the intent of the two works? If characters, for example, or sequences of musical notes seem similar in certain particulars but are, taken as a whole, quite different from each other, the court will be less likely to find infringement.

In considering infringement claims, courts will generally shy away from the type of close textual analysis used in doctoral dissertations; they will look at the two works from the standpoint of an ordinary citizen.[3] This does not mean that they will ignore plagiarism merely because the offending work contains some original matter. A thief is liable for what he has stolen, even if he has possessions of his own; a plagiarist is liable for what he has copied, whether or not he has added to it material of his own invention.[4] This "ordinary observer" test is certainly appropriate for most works. It is not clearly appropriate for highly technical works such as computer programs, and I would not be surprised to see a different standard of analysis develop for such works.

Infringement in the Visual Arts

Where works of visual art are concerned, certain special problems exist. So many piracies that offend our moral sense are not, strictly speaking, infringements. For example, imitation of style, though frequently egregious and irritating, is not infringement unless concrete elements of previous works are plagiarized. The many famous fakes that have been painted in this century, to the extent that they imitate style— brushwork, use of light, type of subject, and so on— and do not actually replicate elements of pictures by the real artist, are not copyright infringements. The fakers may be sued on other grounds—for example, for palming off their works as those of someone else. This is an ordinary action at common law and has nothing to do with copyright.

In the area of visual arts, the problem of subject matter becomes particularly acute. The physical world is of course in the public domain. Any number of artists can paint a face, a harbor, or a street without infringing each other's copyrights. As Justice Oliver Wendell Holmes said, "Others are free to copy the original. They are not free to copy the copy."[5] Does this mean that a photographer has no copyright in a simple unfiltered, unretouched photograph of a natural scene? Almost certainly so. Would the answer be different if the angle, the lighting, or the choice of filter were unusual? The answer to that is less clear.

Difficulties multiply when we talk of arranged subjects. In a well-known case involving a posed photograph of Oscar Wilde, it was held that a photographer's copyright covers any arrangement he makes of natural objects to compose his shot.[6] Should the rule foreclose another photographer from shooting the same subject with different filters and special effects? Or in the realm of painting, should an artist who paints a still life of an identical composition but in a radically different style be considered an infringer? My personal belief is that he should not, but the case has not yet arisen.

Suing the Infringer

An infringer is anyone who violates any of the rights created by law. Suppose you have written a story that someone in Hollywood adapts into a screenplay without your permission. You may sue not only that scriptwriter but also the studio, the film distributors, and the movie theater where the movie is shown.

An infringement suit must be brought in federal court within three years of the time that the infringement took place. Suit on a pre-1978 infringement of common law copyright may still be brought in a state court. This would also apply to any suit based on a work not fixed in a tangible form and so not federally copyrighted.[7] Because the law regards each separate copy, distribution, performance, and so on as a separate infringement, if an infringing book is published in 1980 and you bring suit in 1985, you can receive damages only for copies made or distributed from 1982 on.

As is discussed in detail in chapter 5, for most works of U.S. origin it is necessary to register to sue. And for all works, regardless of origin, registration must be made within three months of first publication or, in the case of unpublished works, must precede the infringement for statutory damages and legal fees to be recoverable.

Only the person who owns the particular right that has been infringed or who is entitled to royalties from it can sue.[8] Suppose that a playwright has sold stage performance rights in his play to a Broadway producer for $200,000 and has licensed United Artists to make a movie version (a derivative work) in return for a royalty of 2 percent of profits. Suppose that another film studio has made an unauthorized film based on the play. Who can sue? United Artists can, because it owns the movie rights, and the author can, because he receives royalties from the movie rights. However, the Broadway producer cannot bring suit even though he may stand to lose box office revenues, because he has no ownership interest in the particular right that has been infringed.

For another example, suppose that a singer sets up a trust for the benefit of her child and transfers to it the right to exploit her sound recordings. In such a case either the trustee or the child can bring suit, because the trustee is the legal owner of the copyright and the child is entitled to the profits.

To return to the example of the play, the fact that the Broadway producer cannot bring suit not necessarily mean that he will never get into court. Quite the contrary. If his interest is likely to be affected by the outcome of the suit, the law requires that he be given notice of it, and he will then be able, at the court's discretion, to join in the fray. The law requires that notice be given to every person whose interest in the work may be affected, and the court may even require that persons whose claims could not possibly be affected also receive notice. All of these people can join in the lawsuit, if the court permits.[9]

Damages in an infringement suit may take the form of actual damages or of what are called "statutory damages." Actual damages can include lost profits, compensation for injury to reputation, compensation for loss of business opportunity (if you can prove it), and, to the extent they exceed the amount of injury actually done, the profits that the infringer has made.[10]

If at any time during the lawsuit it appears that you will not be able to prove actual damages, you can choose instead to receive statutory damages, which will not be less than $200—and that minimum figure will be applied only if the infringer can prove that he had no reason to believe that he was committing an infringement. If he cannot prove this, damages will be not less than $500 and not more than $20,000, unless you in turn can prove that the infringer committed the infringement willfully; in this case you may be awarded as much as $100,000. (For mask works the maximum is $250,000.) These figures are for all infringements of any one work, by each infringer or group of jointly liable infringers. The exact amount of statutory damages is in the discretion of the judge or jury.[11]

In addition to damages you may, in the court's discretion, be reimbursed by the infringer for your court costs and also for your attorney's fees. On the other hand, if you lose your lawsuit and the court decides that in fairness the defendant should be made whole, you may be required to pay the other side's costs and attorneys' fees.[12]

Whether or not you receive damages, you may receive injunctive relief, which is to say that the infringer will be prohibited from any further acts of infringement. Such an injunction is good only against the defendant you have brought to court, although it may serve as a warning to others.

If the infringer infringes willfully and for commercial gain, he can also be prosecuted by the federal government and, if convicted, can be fined or sent to jail or both. From these punishments, of course, you will derive only moral compensation. In the event that you yourself are considering undertaking something you know or strongly suspect to be an infringement, be warned that the criminal penalties are severe: up to $25,000 fine in some cases and up to a year in jail.[13] For record or tape piracy the penalties are even greater.

Fair Use

In infringement suits the two great principles of copyright law almost invariably clash: on one hand the need to protect the financial interests of creators, to make it worth their while to create; on the other hand the need to make each person's addition to the sum of human art and knowledge available for the use of all. From this second principle has evolved the concept of "fair use" of copyrighted material. Fair use, as its name makes no attempt to conceal, is not a fixed navigational point; in any given case much will depend on the judge or jury's instincts.

Underlying the concept of fair use is the problem of economic competition. In English law what we call "fair use" is called "fair dealing"; while that term is inadequate in certain ways, it also captures something important. A use is most likely to be considered permissible if the resulting work does not exploit the commercial value of the original. In this context the quality or nature of the use becomes of primary concern. Congress has officially recognized this in the new statute. The statute adopts four criteria, developed by courts over many decades, by which a use should be judged fair or unfair:

1. The purpose and character of the use, including whether such use is of a commercial nature or is for nonprofit educational purposes.

2. The nature of the copyrighted work.

3. The amount and substantiality of the portion used in relation to the copyrighted work as a whole.

4. The effect of the use on the potential market for or value of the copyrighted work.[14]

Scholarly quotation is one of the most ancient forms of fair use. The law's interest in propagating knowledge requires that critics, news reporters, and similar persons be allowed to quote from works without paying for the privilege. In an interesting recent case the writer of a book on how to win at "Pac-Man" was permitted to use Pac-Man drawings for instructional purposes in the text but not for promotional purposes on the cover.[15] As this case suggests, at some point a quotation will cease to be merely a functioning part of the critical text and begin to stand by itself—to be, in short, a copy. As a general rule a critic or reporter should not quote at any one time more than two or three paragraphs of a book or journal article, a stanza of a poem, or a solitary chart or graph from a technical treatise.

Is it fair use for a scholar to quote someone else's work in support of his own thesis rather than for purposes of criticism? The custom in the publishing industry is to request permission wherever possible in such cases, and this is certainly an honorable approach. However, it is probably not necessary so long as credit is given to the author and the quotation is kept to a minimum.[16] In my view, the publishing industry has become needlessly punctilious about the need for permission to quote short passages. Worthy publishing projects have languished or died as a result. Short quotations are the lifeblood of scholarship and should be presumed lawful except in unusual circumstances.

By the same token, too frequent quotations will not be fair use. For example, a biographer of Stravinsky was recently found to have infringed by excessive reliance on copyrighted statements of the composer to express certain themes. He claimed he used his sub-ject's "radiant, startlingly expressive phrases to make a richer, better portrait of Stravinsky and to make bet-ter reading than a drab paraphrase reduced to bare facts"; the court was not impressed.[17]

These principles of moderation also apply to schol-arly use of visual works. Reproduction of an entire painting, even if reduced and in black and white, would generally infringe the artist's copyright. How-ever, reproduction as necessary to analyze the artist's technique (or to teach Pac-Man strategy) would prob-ably constitute a fair use. Display of works of art in a classroom situation is fair use, as is incidental display or performance in a news broadcast.

The foregoing comments apply to fair use of pub-lished materials; courts have shown less lenience to-ward quotation of unpublished materials. In a recent case involving President Gerald Ford's memoirs, the U.S. Supreme Court found it unfair for *The Nation* to "scoop" *Time* magazine by quoting small excepts from Ford's memoirs before *Time* had published them. The Court noted that the use made by *The Na-tion* was qualitatively significant, but also went out of its way to express a special solicitude for unpub-lished material in general.[18]

Following this lead, the Second Circuit has handed down two opinions of concern to scholars. In the first, it found infringement where an "unofficial" biographer of J. D. Salinger quoted from Salinger's unpublished letters. The court's opinion made much of the fact that the letters were unpublished, even though Salinger's letters were already on deposit in libraries, having been donated by the recipients. Here, as in the Stravinsky case, the defendant had been using quotations more to spice up his prose than to make scholarly points, and so the nature of the use was less than compelling as a defense.

By contrast, in a case involving an unauthorized (and quite critical) biography of L. Ron Hubbard, the founder of Scientology, the author quoted unpublished materials not to "enliven or improve" his book but to "prove a critical point, or to demonstrate a flaw in the subject's character." Yet here too the Second Circuit found the use unfair, notwithstanding strong evidence that the quotations were necessary to prove deceit and venality on the part of Hubbard.[19]

Many in the copyright bar believe that the Second Circuit has gone overboard in its zeal to protect unpublished works. A broad application of the Hubbard ruling could stifle scholarly use of unpublished materials, even where they are used as source materials and not as mere embellishments to a scholar's prose. One judge from the panel vigorously dissented from this part of the ruling, and we may hope that future cases will limit the scope of it. I should note, though, that the Berne Convention can be read to prohibit application of the fair use doctrine to quotations from unpublished works.[20] This may serve, unfortunately, to strengthen the Hubbard rule.

It may take some time for this problem to sort itself out. In the meantime the course of prudence will be to keep even scholarly quotation of unpublished works to a minimum unless the works have passed out of copyright.

Another time-honored fair use, but one less clearly defined, is parody or burlesque. Court after court has wrestled with the question of how much a parodist can appropriate from the original work. To draw too tight a boundary will foreclose the possibility of effective parody, but on the other hand a parody should not be allowed to follow its subject too closely.

One case that in its time caused tremendous controversy is that of *Loew's, Inc. v. Columbia Broadcasting System,* in which Jack Benny was sued for his parody of the movie *Gas Light.*[21] The melodramatic mood in *Gas Light* is so splendidly created that it virtually cries out to be parodied. Jack Benny was not one to pass up such an invitation, and his television parody, entitled *Auto Light,* is a grand example of burlesque. The court, however, found Benny's parody to be infringement because the outline of the plot, the characters, the setting, and some dialogue were copied from the original. Well, you may ask, how can someone burlesque a work without copying these things? Who would even know the object of the satire, or be instructed by it, were these things omitted?

Posterity has not taken a kindly view of the decision of this case. Nonetheless we must recognize that the judge had to grapple with a difficult problem for, as he remarked in another case, "The defense, 'I only burlesqued,' . . . is not per se a defense."[22] In that other case the judge, trying to set forth the criteria by which a parody must be judged, remarked.[23]

In . . . burlesque a part of the content is used to conjure up, at least the general image, of the original. Some limited taking should be permitted under the doctrine of fair use, in the case of burlesque, to bring about this recalling or conjuring up of the original . . . [The parody] may take an incident of the copyrighted story, a developed character (subject to the limited right of an author in certain situations, . . .), a title (subject to the right of protection [against] unfair competition, . . .), some small part of the development of the story, possibly some small amount of the dialogue.

This list is probably correct and useful as far as it goes, but it omits the important question of the quality, the effect of the use, as distinct from the quantity. For if a copy does not compete with the original—and it would be a strange parody that competed with its subject—then more leeway ought to be allowed in the quantity of the copying. This is certainly the intent of Congress in adopting its four criteria of fair use.

On the other hand, the question of competition may tend to obscure one of the other defenses that a parodist can raise: the right of free speech. Where lies the boundary between copyright and freedom of speech, both of which derive from the Constitution? One's first answer is to say that although a citizen may be free to speak, he is not entitled to speak his mind in the same words as his neighbor. He is free to speak the idea, if you will, but not the expression. However, when you consider that "expression" can mean an arrangement of ideas, this answer wears a bit thin. In the end, discussions on this subject are generally reduced to "Well, we know what we mean by free speech, even if we can't put it into words."

Not long ago I nearly had to put it into words. A publisher whom I represent had reprinted two speeches by the Reverend Sun Myung Moon in a book that was a study of Moon's organization and theology. The book, a collection of scholarly pieces by sociologists and students of religion, showed Moon in rather a bad light. Two satellite organizations of Moon's church—The Bicentennial God Bless America Committee and the International Cultural Foundation—sued the publisher, claiming infringement of copyright.

We had a number of technical defenses—prior publication without notice among them—and as our

last line of defense, the First Amendment. I never
learned the strength of any of them, though, because
both plaintiffs settled out of court.

I have often wondered what would have happened
had I raised the issue of the First Amendment. The
precedents were not favorable. One that particularly
worried me was a case involving a group of Catholic
priests who went on tour with their own theologi-
cally corrected version of *Jesus Christ Superstar*.[24]
Among their defenses to an infringement suit was
that the original musical was sick and perverted, and
that therefore they were within their First Amendment rights in defending the true faith. The court did
not agree. Copying verbatim all but a small fraction
of a two- or three-hour musical could not be justified
in the name of freedom of speech and religion.

On the other hand there was the case of Abraham
Zapruder's movies of President Kennedy's assassination. Zapruder, a Dallas dress manufacturer, had
by sheerest chance been aiming his home movie cam-
era at the President's car when the shooting started.
He sold his film to *Time* magazine, which later
brought suit when someone used various film frames
in a book analyzing the assassination. The court in
that case held that the use was in the public interest
and therefore was a fair use.[25] This was not exactly a
First Amendment case, but it came close.

Which precedent would have counted for more in
the Moon case I have no idea. I firmly believe that the
speeches were of great public importance but, more
tellingly, that excerpts or abstracts of them would not
have been sufficient. Taken as a whole, the speeches
were extraordinary jumbles of disconnected plati-
tudes and logical absurdities, and the essence of
what the book's readers deserved to know lay pre-
cisely in that.

So, in full knowledge of the risks, I will undertake to put into words a rule for drawing the line between the First Amendment and copyright. My suggestion is this: Use of a copyrighted work is fair to the extent that the user could not otherwise convey or demonstrate his ideas in exercise of his freedom of speech.

One area in which copyright has recently had to take a back seat is that of copying for private use. Private use has not been the subject of much litigation; we therefore know little about its legality. We know, for example, that an individual cannot go into a museum and photograph a work of art without permission of the copyright owners, even if he only intends the copy for his personal archives.[26] But what about photographing a work of art that he has bought and rightfully owns? Many of us have assumed that this would be acceptable but without more reason than simply a sense of good sportsmanship. The recent Betamax case has been a welcome confirmation.[27]

The case was brought by Universal Pictures and Walt Disney Productions to prevent Sony from marketing the Betamax videocassette player and recorder. Its impact on the movie and television industries promised to be tremendous, so Universal and Disney tried to suppress it at the outset.

To do so, they alleged that by selling these machines Sony was a coinfringer of copyright because it provided infringers with tools of piracy. This in itself was a rather farfetched notion. Although it is true that the Betamax is used largely to tape programs off the air, it is also used to play the very videotape cassettes that the plaintiffs were selling. Moreover, although most television programming is under copyright, many old movies are not, and as time goes by, more and more material will enter the public do-

main. Moreover, as the Supreme Court pointed out
on appeal, the copyright owners of a majority of television programming do not object to taping and may
even be said to encourage it.

Nevertheless the District Court chose to make a reply on the merits and to decide whether copying by
the purchasers of Betamax machines constituted fair
use or infringement. To bring this issue before the
court, Universal and Disney had also sued William
Griffiths, a private user of a Betamax machine. Griffiths was a client of the plaintiffs' law firm, was not
represented by counsel, and the plaintiffs waived all
monetary claims against him. These irregularities the
court also chose to overlook, believing the underlying issue to be important and urgent.

The District Court held for the defendants, and on
appeal the Supreme Court, overruling the Court of
Appeals for the Ninth Circuit by a 5–4 vote, agreed.
In part the decision relied on the fact that the copyright owners of television programs and movies are
already compensated by advertising revenues and so
are not necessarily harmed. As the District Court
noted, Griffiths and other television watchers were
not paying a fee for access to the broadcast. Indeed,
since advertising revenues are the financial under-
pinnings of commercial television, "time-shifting"
(that is, taping a show so as to be able to watch it at
a more convenient time) would seem to benefit,
rather than harm, the copyright owner. The Supreme
Court found time-shifting to be a fair use and rejected the plaintiffs' argument that they should be
able to deny the privilege to their viewers simply
because it was, in "amount and substantiality,"
enormous.

It is hard to say what impact the Betamax case will
have on the law in general. The Supreme Court wrote

a careful and narrow opinion, emphasizing the pe-
culiar facts of the case. For example, the court nimbly
skirted the issue of "librarying" (that is, retaining
copies for an indefinite period), which may more
clearly harm copyright owners by cutting into rerun
revenues. Thus the Supreme Court has not given a
blanket endorsement to home copying. The one principle we can perhaps extract from the case might be
this: For copying, even wholesale copying, in the
confines of one's home to be an infringement, harm
to the copyright owner must be clear.

Even if this is so, it seems clear that use of the copy
must remain personal. No one who has made a copy
for his personal use may distribute it to others. Moreover, even if a given individual's use might otherwise
be considered personal, this would not necessarily
hold true if his copying were part of a community
pattern. For example, a company or college might be
exposed to risk if it came to light that its members
were photocopying works as part of a systematic program for avoiding purchase of the works from the
copyright owner.

How does this rule apply to copying done for an
individual for a fee? A specific exemption is unoffi-
cially given to calligraphers in the congressional report on the new law. (One would not have thought
the calligraphers' lobby was so powerful.) If a calligrapher copies a portion of a work, or even the entirety of a very short work such as a poem, for a
single individual and does not make a another copy
of the same work for any other individual, he will not
be considered an infringer.[28]

Congress also makes an exemption, although un-
officially, for single copies or phonorecords made
without charge for the use of blind persons.[29]

By implication other copying for private customers

is probably not fair use. However, we may never know for certain, because it is not likely to be worth anyone's time and money to sue to prevent it. It is interesting though that the agreement reached several years ago by Gnomon Corporation (a major photocopying company) and the seven publishers that sued it does not mention isolated copying for individuals. The suit between the publishers and Gnomon dealt with a service Gnomon offered under the name of "microprocessing."[30] Gnomon would arrange with university professors to prepare photocopied anthologies of printed works selected by the professors and sell them to students. This was peculiarly blatant infringement, not at all like sporadic copying for private customers.

What about less directly commercial copying? Businesses and law firms, if they wish to comply with the new law, will have to alter many of their traditional practices. For example, it has been commonplace in the past for a company or firm to take out a single subscription to an expensive newsletter and circulate photocopies through the office. This is surely not a fair use. Indeed most business photocopying, because it is made for commercial advantage, is likely to be an infringement of copyright.[31] Recently cases have been brought by publishers against a number of major corporations, including Squibb and American Cyanamid, to stop this and related practices and have been settled on terms very favorable to the publishers. I would strongly recommend that any business that requires multiple copies of works on a regular basis sign on with the Copyright Clearance Center, of Salem, Massachusetts. The CCC offers an "Annual Authorization Service" for a flat yearly fee, which is computed on the basis of the customer's own self-conducted audit.

The two areas of greatest controversy, the areas where a clear need for public access conflicts with an equally clear need to prevent substantial economic loss to authors, are educational use and library photocopying.

Educational Use, Or, Why Johnny Can't Copy

Photocopying of Literary Works and Works of Art

In working on the new law, Congress attempted to establish a code of conduct for educational photocopying. Feelings ran so high on the matter, however, that Congress at last shied away. Instead it gave its unofficial approval, in its report on the statute, to a compromise worked out by the Ad Hoc Committee of Educational Institutions and Organizations on Copyright Law Revision; the Authors League of America, Inc.; and the Association of American Publishers, Inc. Those guidelines are as follows:[32]

I. *Single Copying for Teachers*

A single copy may be made of any of the following by or for a teacher at his or her individual request for his or her scholarly research or use in teaching or preparation to teach a class:

A. A chapter from a book;
B. An article from a periodical or newspaper;
C. A short story, short essay, or short work;
D. A chart, graph, diagram, drawing, cartoon, or picture from a book, periodical, or newspaper.

II. *Multiple Copies for Classroom Use*

Multiple copies (not to exceed in any event more than one copy per pupil in a course) may be made by or for the teacher giving the course for classroom use or discussion, provided that

A. The copying meets the tests of brevity and spontaneity as defined below, and
B. Meets the cumulative effect test as defined below, and
C. Each copy includes a notice of copyright.

Definitions

Brevity

(i) Poetry: (a) A complete poem if less than 250 words and if printed on not more than two pages or, (b) from a longer poem, an excerpt of not more than 250 words.

(ii) Prose: (a) Either a complete article, story, or essay of less than 2,500 words or (b) an excerpt from any prose work of not more than 1,000 words or 10 percent of the work, whichever is less, but in any event a minimum of 500 words.

[Each of the numerical limits stated in "i" and "ii" above may be expanded to permit the completion of an unfinished line of a poem or an unfinished prose paragraph.]

(iii) Illustration: One chart, graph, diagram, drawing, cartoon, or picture per book or per periodical issue.

(iv) "Special" works: Certain works in poetry, prose, or in poetic prose which often combine language with illustrations and which are intended sometimes for children and at other times for a more general audience fall short of 2,500 words in their entirety. Paragraph "ii" above notwithstanding, such "special works" may not be reproduced in their entirety; however, an excerpt comprising not more than two of the published pages of such special work and containing not more than 10 percent of the words found in the text thereof may be reproduced.

Spontaneity

(i) The copying is at the instance and inspiration of the individual teacher, and

(ii) The inspiration and decision to use the work and the moment of its use for maximum teaching effectiveness are so close in time that it would be unreasonable to expect a timely reply to a request for permission.

Cumulative Effect

(i) The copying of the material is for only one course in the school in which the copies are made.

(ii) Not more than one short poem, article, story, essay, or two excerpts may be copied from the same author, nor more than three from the same collective work or periodical volume during one class term.

(iii) There shall not be more than nine instances of such multiple copying for one course during one class term.

[The limitations stated in "ii" and "iii" above shall not apply to current news periodicals and newspapers and current news sections of other periodicals.]

III. *Prohibitions as to I and II Above*

Notwithstanding any of the above, the following shall be prohibited:

A. Copying shall not be used to create or to replace or substitute for anthologies, compilations, or collective works. Such replacement or substitution may occur whether copies of various works or excerpts therefrom are accumulated or reproduced and used separately.

B. There shall be no copying of or from works intended to be "consumable" in the course of study or of teaching. These include workbooks, exercises, standardized tests, and test booklets and answer sheets and like consumable material.

C. Copying shall not
(a) Substitute for the purchase of books, publishers' reprints, or periodicals;
(b) Be directed by higher authority; or
(c) Be repeated with respect to the same item by the same teacher from term to term.

D. No charge shall be made to the student beyond the actual cost of the photocopying.

These guidelines are intended to be not a set of maximum standards but rather a set of minimum standards. If copying for classroom use stays within these guidelines, it will without question be considered fair use. It is conceivable that in a given case a substantial departure from the guidelines might also be considered fair use, by application of the four basic statutory criteria.

Where an anticipated use falls outside the boundaries drawn by the guidelines, it is advisable to seek permission of the copyright owner. One way of doing this is to write directly to whoever is named in the copyright notice on the work. There will of course be works for which no copyright owner is clearly designated. For example, the copyright may be given in the name of a publisher that has gone out of business, or you may be working from a reprinted excerpt that does not bear copyright notice. In any case, unless it is appropriate to write to the publisher, you should write to the Copyright Office to request information regarding the copyright owners. If the Copyright Office is unable to provide guidance, it is likely that reproducing the work would be considered reasonable under the circumstances.

In general, publishers and authors are fairly accommodating in granting permission for educational uses of their works. However, that permission must be explicit. One is not entitled to rely on silence.

"Spontaneity" is a difficult quality to prove or disprove. However, your credibility will decrease, and your liability will increase, if the photocopying that you authorize begins to assume a pattern or if photocopying is "spontaneously" authorized for works that ordinarily would be considered obvious parts of the curriculum.

The requirement that each copy reproduced for classroom use include a notice of copyright should be strictly complied with. Where you are taking an excerpt from a work in such a way that the copyright notice included in the work will not be reproduced, it is your responsibility to ensure that copyright notice in the proper form is put on each copy reproduced. This notice should be identical to that on the work itself. If you are reproducing a previously unpublished work—for example, a friend's manuscript—be certain to obtain his permission for publication. You should put on it proper notice or a legend such as I have suggested for limited publications: "This copy is for private circulation only and may not be used or distributed in any other manner." To be safer yet, you might require that each copy be returned to you at the end of the term.

The guidelines purport to cover single copying for a teacher's personal use. In my opinion they are probably too narrow in this respect. However, copying for personal use must be distinguished from copying in the course of business, and "business" includes teaching duties.

It is important to remember that these guidelines expressly forbid the making of anthologies composed of periodicals and books, even though these may be sold to students at or below cost. They also forbid the copying of consumable items such as workbooks, standardized tests, and answer sheets. Although some flexibility may exist in other part of the guidelines, it is doubtful that any court would sanction much deviation in either of these respects.

Finally, these guidelines do not apply to sheet music or to off-the-air taping of broadcasts. A teacher should seek administrative permission for any activity of this type.

Photocopying of Music for Classroom Use

With respect to music in notational form, a compromise similar to that for literary works and works of art was made by the Music Publishers Association of the United States, Inc.; the National Music Publishers Association, Inc.; the Music Teachers National Association; the Music Educators National Conference; the National Association of Schools of Music; and the Ad Hoc Committee on Copyright Law Revision. The guidelines worked out by this group of organizations are as follows:[33]

A. *Permissible Uses*

1. Emergency copying to replace purchased copies which for any reason are not available for an imminent performance, provided purchased replacement copies shall be substituted in due course.

2. For academic purposes other than performance, single or multiple copies of excerpts of works may be made, provided that the excerpts do not comprise a part of the whole which would constitute a performable unit such as a section, movement, or aria, but in no case more than 10 percent of the whole work. The number of copies shall not exceed one copy per pupil.

3. Printed copies which have been purchased may be edited or simplified provided that the fundamental character of the work is not distorted or the lyrics, if any, altered or lyrics added if none exist.

4. A single copy of recordings of performances by students may be made for evaluation or rehearsal purposes and may be retained by the educational institution or individual teacher.

5. A single [phonorecord] of a sound recording . . . of copyrighted music may be made from sound recordings owned by an educational institution or an individual teacher for the purpose of constructing aural exercises or examinations and may be retained by the educational institution or individual teacher . . . [This guideline deals only with copyright in the music itself and not with copyright in the sound recording; the recording industry was not involved in negotiating these guidelines. How-

ever, I believe that the identical standard would apply to the sound recording copyright as well.]

B. *Prohibitions*

1. Copying to create or replace or substitute for anthologies, compilations, or collective works.

2. Copying of or from works intended to be "consumable" in the course of study or of teaching such as workbooks, exercises, standardized tests, and answer sheets and like material.

3. Copying for the purpose of performance, except as in A(1) above.

4. Copying for the purpose of substituting for the purchase of music, except as in A(1) and A(2) above.

5. Copying without inclusion of the copyright notice which appears on the printed copy.

Like the other photocopying guidelines, these are intended to define not the outer limits of fair use but minimum standards within which use may safely be assumed to be fair.

Guideline A(3) should not be understood to prohibit editing a piece of music in one's personal scholarly pursuits or as a classroom exercise. However, no teacher should make substantial revisions of a piece of music and distribute copies of the edited version or cause it to be performed, in class or elsewhere.

With respect to guideline A(4), no copyright owner's permission need be sought to sell recordings of student performances if the works performed have been previously recorded for public sale by someone else. The compulsory license for phonorecords would apply here.

The prohibition against the making of anthologies and the requirement that proper copyright notice be placed on each copy made for classroom use apply to sheet music just as to other printed works.

Copying of
Computer
Programs

None of the foregoing guidelines applies to copying of computer software. I am told that unauthorized copying of floppy disks is becoming a widespread practice in many schools. Any such copying is clearly beyond the bounds of fair use and should be avoided, unless of course the copies are strictly for archival purposes.

Classroom
Performance or
Display

It is permissible for teachers and their students to perform or display any work in class so long as the class is held on campus or, if off campus, in classroom-type circumstances and classroom-type surroundings. However, you cannot show a motion picture or other audiovisual work or display individual images from such a work if you know or suspect that the copy you use was not lawfully made.

Special
Exemption:
Institutions for
the Deaf and
Hearing
Impaired

In the Conference Committee Report on the new statute, Congress adopted the view of Congressman Robert Kastenmeier, one of its leading copyright authorities, that fair use covers certain uses of television programs by nonprofit educational institutions for the deaf and hearing impaired. Congressman Kastenmeier had said that such an institution can make an off-the-air copy of a television program, make a captioned version of it, perform that version within the confines of the institution, and lend it to similar institutions for similar use. This use will be fair use only if it is noncommercial in every respect and if its purpose is to contribute to the student's learning environment.[34]

**Library
Copying**

Among the issues of greatest concern in this area is that of copying for reserve use. Unfortunately Congress has not spoken on this matter. I believe that photocopying a chapter or similar small portion of a work for placement on reserve is a fair use, but this is no more than an informed guess.

The law does, however, specifically exempt from liability certain copying done in libraries.[35] (For convenience I use the word *library* to include archives.) The exemption is limited to circumstances in which the library making the copy owns the work as part of its own collection, only one copy is made, no charge is made for the copy beyond recovery of costs, and the copy made by the library bears the copyright notice that the work itself bears.

Subject to these limitations it is permissible for a library to copy works under four circumstances:

1. If the work is unpublished and a copy is necessary for purposes of preservation and security. To qualify under this exemption, the copy must be in "facsimile form." The meaning of this phrase is extremely broad—it includes, for example, microfilm—but it does not include putting a work into machine-readable language for storage in an information system. What Congress had in mind when it made this distinction is unclear. A reasonable guess is that facsimile form is any form that stores the work in more or less its given medium. Microfilm qualifies because it reproduces the printed page; a computer database does not qualify because it stores a printed work by means of electromagnetic impulses.

2. If the work is unpublished and another library requests a copy for its own collection. Here, too, the copy must be in facsimile form.

3. If the work is published and the copy is needed to replace one that has been damaged, lost, or stolen, or is deteriorating. However, the library must first have made a reasonable effort to obtain an unused replacement at a fair price. The effort to find an unused replacement at a fair price would involve resort-

ing to commonly known trade sources in the United States, to the publisher, and to any other copyright owner (if the owner can be located at the address listed in any copyright registration that has been made of the work). It will also involve checking with any central photocopying service that is authorized to reproduce the work. Certain additional efforts beyond these may be regarded as reasonable in a particular case but will be unnecessary in most cases. A copy made under this exemption must be a facsimile copy.

4. If the copy has been requested by a user of the library or by another library on behalf of one of its users. A copy made under this exemption must become the property of the user, and the library making the copy must have no reason to believe that it will be used for purposes other than private study, scholarship, or research. The exemption applies only if the library prominently displays a copyright warning notice at the place where patrons order copies and on its order forms.[36] The form and placement of notice are prescribed by regulations, which are reproduced in appendix E. The exemption, moreover, is limited in subject matter; it does not apply to musical works, to pictorial or graphic works (except when used as illustrations of literary works), to sculptural works, or to motion pictures or other audiovisual works. Nor does it apply to any more than a small part of a work (meaning, in the case of a periodical or other collective work, one solitary contribution), unless a copy of the work cannot be obtained at a fair price. To try to obtain a copy of the work, you must make an investigation. Furthermore, this exemption does not apply if the library is systematically distributing photocopies of copyrighted material, except where copies are not obtainable in the market at a fair price.

What is "systematic" copying? With respect to user requests, copying is probably systematic if it is available to any user with no questions asked. Copying done on a case-by-case basis only, with a clear requirement that there be some special need for it, will probably be all right. With respect to interlibrary arrangements, copying is systematic if it is so great or continuous as to substitute, in practical effect, for a purchase or subscription. The National Commission on New Technological Uses for Copyrighted Works has developed a set of specific guidelines to give flesh to this rather bare definition.[37] These guidelines, which have the unofficial blessing of Congress, are summarized briefly:

• With respect to periodical issues less than five years old, one library may obtain from another no more than five copies of material from any given periodical—as opposed to any given issue of a periodical—in any given calendar year.

• With respect to material other than periodicals, one library may obtain from another no more than five copies of or from any given work in any one calendar year.

• No guidelines are given for periodical issues published more than five years before the date of the request.

• If the requesting library has on order or in its collection the item that it wants copied, but does not have the item in its possession at the time and cannot reasonably repossess it at the time, the copy made at its request will not count toward the maximum number of permissible copies. For example, if a library has a book out at the binder, it can request a copy from another library without using up any of its five-copy allowance.

• A library cannot satisfy a request unless it is accom-

panied by a representation from the requesting
library that the request conforms with these guidelines, if these guidelines apply.
• Every library must keep on file for three years each
request it makes to another library.

None of these library exemptions applies if a library has reason to believe that its copying is, or is
part of, a concerted reproduction of distribution of
multiple copies of the same material. A "related and
concerted" reproduction can take place over a period
of time and need not involve one single user, but can
be with respect to a number of different users; it can
also be found where a copy is requested by a group
for the separate use of its various members.

None of the numerical restrictions on the library
exemption applies to videotape copies of news programs. A library may tape news broadcasts off the air
and lend them to scholars and researchers for research purposes. Presumably it may also lend to
other libraries for the same purposes. However, the
term *news programs* is fairly narrow. It does not apply
to documentaries (except "documentary programs
involving news reporting") or to magazine-format
shows or other public-affairs broadcasts dealing with
subjects of general interest.[38] For example, the special
same-day reports prepared by the major networks on
the downing of the Pan Am jet over Scotland were
"news programs"; segments of "60 Minutes" are not.

None of these exemptions either restricts or ex-
pands the rights of fair use. It is conceivable that in
some cases the library would be safe in going beyond
the limitations described here if, in its considered
judgment, the activity it contemplated was a fair use.
On the other hand, the fact that a library may be exempt from liability in no way relieves an individual
user who requests a copy from the library if the mak-

ing of that copy would not be a fair use. In short these exemptions are for the benefit of the library and its personnel, not for persons making use of the library.

None of these exemptions overrules any contractual understanding a library may have with a copyright owner.

Finally, libraries are not liable for wrongful copying done on public machines if they have placed on the machines a warning against copyright infringement (See appendix E.)[39]

The Sovereign Immunity Scandal

As of 1989 an odd exception to the law of infringement had emerged in various court decisions. To the surprise of copyright scholars and the distress of copyright owners, it has been held that no state government can be sued for damages in copyright infringement without its own consent.[40] This "sovereign immunity" defense is not available to the U.S. government, or indeed to cities and towns, but only to states. It rests on the Eleventh Amendment to the U.S. Constitution, which limits the jurisdiction of federal courts over state governments. It appears that Congress does in fact have the power to subject the states to that jurisdiction where copyright is concerned; the cases have held only that Congress did not do so explicitly enough.

One may doubt whether sovereign immunity in any form, at least where there is an active taking of property (which is what copyright infringement amounts to), is acceptable in a democracy. And to the extent that these decisions are based on technical construction of the U.S. Copyright Act, they seem to me implausible. The whole matter is made yet more odd by the fact that individual state officials remain liable for infringement, and that state governments can still be *enjoined* from future infringement even if they cannot be sued for past infringement.

Nonetheless the sovereign immunity defense will, if allowed to stand, seriously affect educational and library photocopying, copying of computer software especially at state research universities, and other important copyright markets. As of July 1989, Congress was actively considering legislation to overrule the courts. It is to be hoped that this legislation succeeds.

9

So far I have dealt with the law that will apply to works created in 1978 or thereafter. In all respects but one it is also the law that will apply to works created but neither published nor registered with the Copyright Office as unpublished works before 1978. (The previous federal statute permitted registration of certain works of the performing and visual arts prior to publication.) The one difference has to do with duration of the copyright term. The law makes a special provision for works in this category: no copyright for such a work can expire before December 31, 2002, and, furthermore, if the work is published before that date, its copyright will not expire before December 31, 2027.

Works that were published or registered before 1978 are governed by a different set of rules. Although in many respects the new law will apply to those works, several fundamental provisions of the old system that have otherwise been discarded will also apply. Since these works are by far the majority of works in existence and will be for many years to come, it is important to know those portions of the old law that are still of concern.

Publication and Notice under the Old Law

Chief among the basic premises of the old copyright system was the division between statutory copyright and common law copyright, a division based on the concept of publication. Common law copyright was, in essence, the right of "first publication"; it entitled its owner to exploit his work exclusively and in almost any manner for an unlimited period of time, so long as he did not publish it, and it entitled him to be the first to publish the work. Beyond that the common law would not go; once you published your work, you either assumed the mantle of federal statutory copyright, or, if you did not properly protect yourself, you forfeited your work to the public domain.

At the moment of first publication within the United States, notice became crucial. (Notice or lack of notice in foreign publication had no effect one way or the other.)[1] If you affixed proper notice to the work, you automatically secured statutory copyright. If you failed to affix proper notice, your work went into the public domain.

Requirements for Notice under the Old Law

These requirements[2] were much the same as they are today, with certain important differences:

1. The date of first publication was not required on any copies except printed copies of literary, musical, or dramatic works, and phonorecords (called "reproductions" in the old law) of sound recordings.

2. On the first publication, only the name of the copyright proprietor could be used. Thus on first publication the person whose name appeared in the notice had to be the owner of the entire copyright.

3. The full name of the copyright owner had to be used except on visual works and sound recordings; abbreviations, trademarks, and other symbols were not acceptable. If the name given in the notice on a

visual work was in fact a trademark or other symbol, the full and proper name had to appear somewhere, even if only on the bottom or back of the work.

4. Placement of the notice was strictly regulated. In the case of any printed work other than a periodical, notice had to be placed on the title page or the page immediately following. In the case of a periodical, it had to be placed on the title page or on the first page of text of each separate issue or under the title heading. In the case of sheet music or other printed musical work, it went on the title page or the first page of music. And in the case of phonorecords and visual works, it went in some "reasonable" place. ("Reasonable" had basically the same meaning as under the new law.)

5. Any defect in the notice, including omission of any part of proper notice, caused the work to be treated as if notice had been omitted entirely. There were only two exceptions. If, by accident or mistake, the year given in the notice was earlier than the true year of first publication, the copyright term simply began in the earlier year, and if, by accident or mistake, the year given was later than the true year by no more than a year, the fault was overlooked, at least where no innocent person, relying on the faulty notice, had begun to exploit the work thinking it to be in the public domain.[3] (This charitable approach to notices defective by only one year was a comparatively recent development.)

Under the old law, if notice was omitted or given improperly, copyright was lost. There were not all the special indulgences provided in the new law for registration within five years, and so on; what was done could not be undone. There were only two exceptions. First, omission of proper notice had no effect if the copies or phonorecords were distributed without the authority of the copyright owner. Second, omission from a very small number of copies, if caused by accident or mistake (other than mistake as to what the law required), did not affect the copyright; however, an innocent person acting in the belief that the work was in the public domain (having been misled by the lack of notice) would not be liable for damages and could be enjoined from further infringement only if the copyright proprietor agreed to reimburse him for his out-of-pocket expenses.

Notice under the New Law for Works First Published Before 1978

The new law provides that works first published before 1978 may continue to abide the old formalities of notice. Any new copies or phonorecords of those works can bear either the notice that was acceptable under the old law or that required by the new law. However, the reverse is not true. If copies or phonorecords distributed before 1978 did not carry notice that was proper at the time, the consequences will be governed by the old law, even though the notice might be permissible by post-1977 standards.[4]

Copyright Ownership under the Old Law

Indivisibility and the Periodicals Problem

The problem of notice brought into play another important principle of the old law, one that the new law has gone to great lengths to eliminate: that copyright ownership was indivisible. You could give other people licenses to use your work in one way or another, but you could not sell them any absolute right under the copyright; the only absolute transfer you could make was of the entire copyright as an undivided whole. This concept caused particular difficulties in the area of notice because the old statute specifically stated that notice at the time of first publication had to be in the name of the copyright owner or it would be considered to be no notice at all, and the work would go into the public domain. Thus if you gave a magazine permission to make first publication of a story, but neither transferred copyright ownership to the magazine nor insisted that separate notice be inserted in your own name, copyright notice in the name of the magazine would not protect your copyright.

Over the course of time courts made many inroads in this rather rigid formalism, primarily by finding that an author had in fact conveyed all of his rights to the magazine, but that the magazine held them in trust for him, with a promise to reconvey them after publication. In 1970 the Second Circuit Court of Appeals (generally a bellwether court in copyright matters) simply abandoned the whole doctrine of indivisibility, at least as far as notice was concerned.[5] Thus if you made any sale or license of magazine rights after 1970, the chances are great, even though a court will be obliged to apply the old law to your case, that you will be protected by whatever notice was put on the magazine as a whole. Indeed in most cases the Second Circuit's view could probably be applied to pre-1970 situations as well.

Presumably this 1970 opinion swept away another old doctrine as applied to periodicals: that if a publisher, having secured copyright in its own name, conveyed its rights to someone else, the name in any copyright notice on the work could not be changed until the conveyance had been recorded with the Copyright Office.[6]

The same rules applied to derivative works and so-called composite works. (This term, roughly similar to the new term *collective works*, has vanished from the law as of 1978.) Movie rights contracts, for example, were often treated as licenses rather than sales, and so theoretically copyright notice in the name of the producer did not protect the copyright in any unpublished story licensed to the producer; fortunately, however, this problem seems to have surfaced very seldom in the movie context. Should a case come to trial now on a pre-1978 movie rights license, it is more than likely that a court will ignore the old doctrine of indivisibility and hold that notice in the name of the studio or the producer is not defective.

Another quirk of the indivisibility doctrine, and a particularly odd one, caused a great deal of mischief for many decades. This was the assumption that sale of an unpublished manuscript, painting, or other work carried with it the sale of common law copyright in the work unless the seller expressed some clear intent to the contrary.[7] This rule was reversed by statute (at least as to works of fine art, though not as to manuscripts) in New York in 1966 and by statute in California in 1976.[8] ("Fine art" in the New York law meant paintings, sculpture, drawings, or graphic art. In California it meant any kind of visual art.) It is not clear, however, what would happen if the case were to arise now concerning a sale carried out in either of those states before their laws were changed or in any state other than California and New York before 1978. Perhaps the old rule would be ignored, but I can offer no guarantee.

Works Made for Hire

The old law was much looser than the new law in its approach to works made for hire. Whether a work fell under the rule depended entirely on the intent of the persons involved. This meant that most commissioned works were regarded as works made for hire, but it meant also that an employer and employee could agree to waive the rule and could do so either orally or in writing.

There was some disagreement in the case of a commissioned work as to whether the commissioning party was to be treated as the author or only as the owner of the first-term copyright. The latter view seems to be prevailing at the moment.[9] However, since the intent of the persons involved is a factor here as well, the question is open to litigation.

Whether a work was made for hire, and whether in the case of a commissioned work the hirer got the entire copyright or only the first-term copyright, will be particularly important questions in the context of termination rights. They will also continue to affect the ownership of renewal rights.

Joint Works

In most respects the old law governing joint works does not differ from the new law. However, the new law has rejected one doctrine that still has validity for pre-1978 works. This doctrine, first stated in what is known as the "12th Street Rag" case, is that intent to create a joint work can arise after one of the joint authors has already completed his part of the work.[10] Euday L. Bowman had composed "12th Street Rag" as an instrumental piano solo and then assigned his rights to a publisher. The publisher commissioned lyrics for it. Bowman had no notion of setting words to his music; it was entirely the publisher's idea; nonetheless the court held that the resulting song was a joint work, giving the lyricist copyright in the music as well as the lyrics.

The court stressed that what mattered was the intent of whoever owned the copyright at the time the contributions were brought together, not the intent of either author at the time of creation. Effectively it permitted someone to give up exclusive rights in a work by allowing it to be incorporated in a joint work. The doctrine would not extend, for example, to someone who sold movie rights in a novel to a producer, for in that case the seller does not intend that the novel will become merely a part of a movie.

Limited as it may be, this "12th Street Rag" doctrine will continue to affect royalty rights and renewal rights even under the new law, and will also have repercussions for termination rights under the new law. It should therefore be taken into account whenever you are dealing with a work that can be interpreted as a joint work.

Special Rules for Pre-1978 Sound Recordings and Phonorecords

Because under pre-1978 copyright law a thing from which a work could not be visually perceived was not an infringing "copy" of the work,[11] special rules arose concerning tapes and records, or what the new law calls phonorecords.

Until 1972 no protection at all was given by federal law to sound recordings. It was left to the states to pass record-piracy laws, and many of them did.[12] However, as of February 15, 1972, federal law was amended so as to apply to sound recordings published on or after that date. The new law largely carries this forward, with certain changes in the terms of the compulsory license. But sound recordings made before February 15, 1972 will continue to be protected by state piracy laws until February 15, 2047, after which date they will be protected by federal laws or not at all.[13]

What of the underlying musical works? Here there was great uncertainty. For years many courts believed that even though an unauthorized record or tape was not a copy that could infringe a musical work, a record or tape of a musical work nonetheless published the work and had to bear copyright notice covering the music. Many copyright lawyers disagreed and advised composers who were their clients accordingly. As a result many recordings were issued bearing no notice of copyright. Were the musical works put into the public domain? No one really knows.

In 1973 an authoritative opinion came down holding that if a record was not a copy for one purpose, it would not be a copy for another purpose.[14] But whether this eminently sensible decision clarified the law retroactively or only for the few remaining years of the old statute is not clear. My advice is to regard any musical work published in a pre 1973 recording as being still protected by copyright, regardless of whether it bears a copyright notice.

Copyright Term under the Old Law

The second major area in which the old law will continue to exert an influence for many decades to come is that of copyright duration, and particularly copyright renewal.

Under the old law copyright lasted for a twenty-eight–year term, but, if registered, could obtain a second twenty-eight–year term. Thus, for example, a copyright secured on May 12, 1932 would have run through May 11, 1960. If a copyright was not renewed in the last year of its first term, it went into the public domain. If it was renewed, it went into the public domain at the end of the second term. However, during the years that Congress was deliberating over the new statute, the expiration of second-term copyright was repeatedly postponed. Any work still in its renewal term on September 19, 1962 remained covered as of January 1, 1978.

The United States' joining the Berne Convention has no retroactive effect on this. Thus, although registration is no longer required for non-U.S. works protected under the Berne Convention, such works, if published before 1961, must still be registered and renewed in order to obtain a second term of copyright.

Renewal of copyright was accomplished by filing an application for renewal with the Copyright Office in the last year of the original twenty-eight–year copyright term. Remember that if the notice on the work gave a date that was earlier than the true date of publication, the twenty-eight–year term ran from the date of notice, not from the date of first publication. This application could be filed by anyone, or on behalf of anyone, who was or might be entitled to the renewal term. In most cases the person entitled had to be alive on the day that the renewal term was to begin or the renewal copyright would go to someone else. The right to renew was thus a mongrel sort of creation—rather like the termination right created by the new law—in that it was a right you possessed only as long as you lived. If you were, say, a composer of music and had copyright in a musical score, you could file for a renewal in the last year of your first copyright term. But if you died before that last year was up, the right to renew your copyright passed to your heirs, and someone who had purchased the renewal copyright from you was out of luck.

The provision for renewal, like that for termination under the new law, was designed to protect artists from themselves—and from the impossibility of knowing the true value of a work when it is first created—by giving them a chance to regain their copyrights after twenty-eight years. Unfortunately this noble purpose never was fulfilled, for those who wished to exploit artists, and those artists who preferred a dollar in hand to an uncertain hope of future riches, began to arrange sales and licenses of the renewal term in advance. (Generally these sales had to be explicit to be enforceable. A sale by an author of "all my right, title, and interest" in a work was usually interpreted not to include a sale of the renewal copyright.)[15] Moreover, because the sale would be worthless if the artist died before having a chance to renew his copyright, it became common for spouses and children of artists to make ends meet by selling in advance whatever rights they might get if the artist died prematurely.[16]

Sales by authors and their families of the renewal term copyright have not always been upheld. If the seller can show that the sale was made under "such coercion of circumstances that enforcement would be unconscionable," a court will not enforce the bargain.[17] This is part of a growing tendency on the part of courts to invalidate unconscionable contracts of all kinds, and is not strictly a doctrine of copyright law.

Ownership of Copyright after Renewal

The basic rule was that copyright for the second term did not become anyone's property until the term actually began. At that point it became the property of whoever was by law entitled to renewal, but only if that person had actually applied for renewal (or if an application had been filed on this behalf). The validity of the application thus depended on the applicant's surviving until he became entitled to the copyright renewal. What made this provision particularly dangerous was that if the only person or persons who applied for renewal died before the commencement of the renewal term, the work would go into the public domain. To avoid this result, it became the general practice for everyone who might conceivably be entitled to file a claim for renewal to do so, just in case the author died prematurely.

The question of who was entitled to the renewal copyright was rather complicated. If an author died before the end of his first copyright term, the right to renew went to his surviving spouse and his children, or as many of them as were living, as a group. Any one of them or all of them could then apply for renewal, and when the renewal term began, the copyright would belong as of that moment to as many of the family as were alive at the time. (The surviving spouse retained the renewal right regardless of remarriage.)[18] For example, if a novelist died before renewal term began, leaving a husband and three children, any one of those four persons could apply for renewal, and to be safe, all four would apply. If all four were alive on the date that the renewal term began, each of them received a 25 percent share in the new copyright. But if before that date one of those four died, the other three would take the second term's copyright in equal shares of one-third each. From that point on the owners of the various shares were regarded as tenants in common. Each of them could make a transfer of the copyright, but would have to account to the other owners for a fair share of the profits.

The law spoke only of children; more remote descendants were not mentioned. (Whether illegitimate children could take advantage of the statute used to depend on state law regarding the rights of illegitimate children, but it appears that illegitimate children can renew under the new law.)[19] The omission of more remote descendants meant that if the novelist in the example died leaving no family except grandchildren, the renewal copyright would go to the executor of her estate, who would then pass it on to whoever was entitled to receive it by the terms of her will. If the novelist left no will, the copyright would go to her next of kin, who in this case would be the grandchildren. If, however, the novelist was survived only by her husband and her grandchildren, the husband would get the entire copyright, and the grandchildren would get nothing. If she was survived by a child and by children of a deceased child, those grandchildren would not even take a *per stirpes* share. The rule seems harsh, but it has never been changed.

Because an application for renewal could be made "on behalf of" the person or corporation entitled to renewal, anyone who wished to could apply for renewal, as long as he did so in the name of the person entitled by law to renew. For example, if the author had sold his right to the renewal term, he was still entitled by law to file the claim for renewal, but people who purchased the renewal copyright from an author rarely relied on the author to make the renewal claim; instead they filed the claim themselves on his behalf. Thus also a magazine contributor whose contribution had been registered only as part of a magazine issue could still apply for renewal, as long as he did so in the name of the owner of copyright in the magazine.[20] In this manner he could protect his renewal copyright without having to depend on the publisher.

Renewal of Joint Works

In the case of a joint work, any one of the authors could file for renewal because each of them had a right to treat the entire copyright as his own, although he had to account to his co-owners for any profits he made by doing so. This theory, if taken to its logical conclusion, ought to have meant that if only one of several joint authors obtained renewal of the copyright, he was the one who got the renewal term, subject to his obligation to account to his co-owners. However, the general rule has been to give all of the joint authors full ownership of the renewal term.[21]

Exceptions to these General Rules

There were four exceptions to the rule that an author of his surviving family, or his heirs, were entitled to the renewal copyright. For four categories of works, ownership of the original copyright brought with it entitlement to the renewal copyright as well.

The first category was that of so-called posthumous works. What was a posthumous work? For a long time it was believed that a posthumous work was one not published before the author's death. However, though this definition fit in with familiar usage and conventional wisdom, it had the effect of disinheriting the author's spouse and children, for it meant that if an author before his death sold his copyright to someone else and died before publication, the purchaser would own the renewal right without having paid a dime for it. Responding to this clear inequity, the Second Circuit Court of Appeals in 1975 decreed that henceforth it would regard as posthumous only works in which the author had not, during his life, made any contract for exploitation of his copyright by publication, performance, or otherwise.[22] This meant that the only person who would have the right to renew copyright in a posthumous work would be the person who inherited the copyright from the author. That of course still left it open to the author to bequeath his common law copyright by will to some unrelated person, but the practical effect of the new rule has generally been a tremendous benefit to the families of authors. This definition of posthumous works has been adopted by Congress for all renewals made after January 1, 1978.[23]

The second category was of works published without separate notice in a magazine or other "composite work." The author of the contribution did not possess the renewal right unless his work bore a separate copyright notice.[24] However, the practical significance of this was minimal, because if the publisher held the original copyright in trust for the author, as courts have recently tended to declare, it would also hold the renewal copyright in trust.

The third and fourth categories were closely related. The third comprised works made for hire. As noted above, though, where such works were *commissioned,* some courts have awarded the renewal term to the creator. The fourth comprised works in which copyright originally belonged to a corporate body (for example, a company, a board of trustees, or a charitable society). Since this would not be so if the corporate body was not itself the author of the work, in most cases this fourth exception simply overlapped with the work-made-for-hire exception.

Effect of Renewal on Derivative Works

Because a renewal term of copyright is a clean slate or, as some courts say, a "new estate," licenses that were given in the first term generally become null and void. The only possible exception to this rule is for derivative works made under license during the first term.

The Second Circuit has held that the copyright owner of such a work may continue to exploit it during the renewal term. This view is in keeping with the new termination doctrine, that a derivative work may continue to be exploited after statutory termination of the license (see chapter 3). However, it is really not in keeping with the law of renewal copyrights. The better view, expressed by the Ninth Circuit, is that the derivative work cannot be exploited without a license specifically covering the renewal term.[25]

Here again, alas, a split has developed between circuits that makes geography a determinant of the ownership of rights. We must hope that the Second Circuit reverses itself or that the Supreme Court over-rules it.

Renewal under the New Law

Any pre-1978 work must be renewed in exactly the same way, and to the benefit of exactly the same persons, as it would have been under the old law. There is a new and different renewal application form (form RE), and the fee for renewal has gone up to $6, but otherwise the old law carries over, with only a few substantial changes.[26]

Renewing a Group of Works

As I have mentioned, under the new law it is possible for an author to register a number of contributions to collective works on the same form. The new law has a similar provision where renewal is concerned. In the case of the works of an individual author, renewal registration may be made on a single form and for a single fee if these conditions are met:

• If the renewal claimant or claimants are the same for each work. For example, if a magazine owns two of the renewal rights and the author's family own the other two, the same registration form cannot be used for all four works.

• If the basis of the claim is the same for each work. This will be the case in all but a very few circumstances. An example to the contrary would be if the publisher is entitled to renew some works because their renewal terms were assigned to it by the author and entitled to renew others because they were works made for hire; in both cases the publisher is the proper renewal claimant, but it cannot use the same form to renew all of these works.

• If the works were all copyrighted at the time of their first publication, either by separate notice and registration or by virtue of a copyright notice having been affixed to the periodical issue as a whole, regardless of whether that issue was registered.

• If all the works were published in one calendar year.

• If the application identifies each work and states the name and date of the periodical issue in which it was first published.[27]

Length of Renewal Term

The new law has lengthened the renewal term for pre-1978 works.[28] It might seem unfair that authors of works copyrighted before 1978 should not get the benefit of the life-plus-fifty term, but Congress felt that altering the structure of existing copyrights to that extent would upset the financial expectations of people who had invested in them and would cause numerous other difficulties and contradictions. Instead Congress added nineteen years to the renewal term of copyright for works in their first term as of January 1, 1978. Those works, if renewed, are now protected for a total of seventy-five years from the year of first publication.

The renewal term for works that were already in their second term when the new law went into effect, or for which a timely renewal application was still pending on December 31, 1977, has also been lengthened by nineteen years. Those works too will thus be protected for a total of seventy-five years from the year of first publication.

In all cases the copyright term for pre-1978 works that were still under copyright on January 1, 1978 runs through the end of the *calendar* year in which it would otherwise expire. This is a great improvement over prior law.

The addition of nineteen years is intended to benefit authors, not the people to whom they may have sold their rights. To ensure that this will in fact be the result, the new law has adopted a procedure for terminating renewal term grants, and that includes not only grants of the renewal right but also any grant or license that applies to the renewal term. The procedure is similar in most respects to that for terminating transfers of post-1977 copyrights.

Terminating Pre-1978 Grants of Renewal Rights

The right to terminate transfers of renewal copyright[29] applies only to transfers made before January 1, 1978 of copyright in works published before that date. No grant or license concerning the renewal term made after December 31, 1977 can be terminated. The right is not available for works made for hire, and it does not affect grants made by will or grants of rights in foreign countries. Furthermore it affects only the nineteen-year extension period, not the basic twenty-eight–year renewal term.

Grants Made by Persons Other than the Author

It is now possible for an author's spouse or children to terminate grants of renewal rights that they have made. It is also possible for them to terminate any grant that takes effect during the renewal term.

Termination must be made by all of the grantors who are still alive. Thus if three children joined in making a grant of renewal rights and two of them die, the remaining child can effect termination all by himself. But if all three children are still alive, all three must join in making the termination.

The heirs of a deceased grantor other than the author have no termination rights. Thus, in my example, if two children die before having a chance to take part in the termination, the remaining child is the only person who can effect termination; a deceased child's children have no rights in this respect. Nor do they have any rights once termination has been carried out. However, from the moment that the copyright reverts to the persons who terminated the grant, which it does on the date the termination becomes effective, it becomes property; it is no longer personal to the grantor but can be inherited. Thus if a child dies after taking part in the termination, his heirs will get an equal share of the copyright. This distinction seems unfair, but it is nonetheless the law.

Grants Made by the Author

Termination of grants of renewal rights made by the author may be made by him alone, if he is living. If the author is dead, the termination right is owned and may be exercised by his family. His spouse has the entire right if there are no children or grandchildren; his children and grandchildren have the entire right if there is no spouse; if there are both a spouse and children or grandchildren, the spouse has half the termination right and the children and grandchildren have the other half, divided among them in equal shares *per stirpes*. The share of a deceased child can be exercised only by a majority of his children. In short, apportionment of the termination rights is identical to that provided for grants of copyright in post-1977 works.

Grants of Renewal in Joint Works

Any author who joined in a grant of rights regarding the renewal term may terminate the grant to the extent of his share of the rights. (If he is dead, his termination right may be exercised by his family.) This provision for joint works differs substantially from the rule covering grants of copyright in post-1977 works. The rule in the latter case is that a majority of authors who signed the original grant must join in giving notice of termination; but in the case of grants concerning the renewal term made before January 1, 1978, each of the joint authors can terminate his own individual share of the grant. This may work some hardship in years to come, for it appears that if one of the joint owners pulls out, he can make a grant to someone else, and the person who has the original grant will be stuck paying royalties to the other joint authors but without any longer having an exclusive license.

Ownership of Copyright after Termination of a Grant Made by the Author

When a grant made by an author is terminated, the copyright reverts on the date termination becomes effective. However, it does not necessarily revert to the persons who made the termination, as is the case for grants made by someone other than the author. The reversion goes to the author or, if he is deceased, to his family in the same proportions as the termination rights but without regard to who signed or did not sign the termination notice. For example, a child who did not sign the termination notice still receives a proportionate share of the copyright when it reverts.

Any new grant of a right that has reverted in this manner is valid only if it is in writing and only if it is signed by the same number of persons, and by persons representing the same proportion of ownership, as were required to carry out termination. This is so whether the new grant is exclusive or nonexclusive. (A new grant of a right originally granted by persons other than the author does not have to meet these number and proportion requirements.)

An example may help to demonstrate these rules. Suppose that termination rights in a work are owned 50 percent by the author's widow and 25 percent by each of two daughters. Termination would have to be carried out by at least two persons (the widow and at least one daughter). At the time of notice the right to reversion of the copyright vests in the widow and daughters in the same proportions. Suppose that one of the daughters then dies, leaving her share of the copyright to her alma mater. (She was able to make this bequest because ownership of the copyright had vested in her.) For a new grant of the copyright to be valid, it must be signed by at least two persons, who must represent at least the same percentage of the right as was required for termination. But they need not be the same persons who terminated the original grant. Thus the statute is satisfied if the grant is signed by the widow and the college.

The new grant binds and benefits even those who did not participate in it. Thus the daughter who does not sign the new grant is still legally bound by it, and the buyer is obligated to pay her a share of the royalties.

Mechanics for Terminating a Renewal Term Grant

The following rules apply to all terminations of renewal right grants, whether the grants were made by the author or by his family:[30]

1. Termination may take effect at any time during the five-year-period beginning either fifty-six years from the date that copyright in the work was first secured, or January 1, 1978, whichever date is later.

2. Notice of termination, which must be in writing and signed by all persons whose consent is required for termination, must be given not more than ten years and not fewer than two years before the date that termination is to take effect.

3. A copy of the notice must be recorded in the Copyright Office before the date of termination, or the termination becomes null and void. The fee for recording is $10, plus $.50 for every page over six.

4. As with the termination of grants of post-1977 copyrights, no new grant, and no agreement to make a new grant, can be made until the date termination becomes effective, except that renegotiation of an ex-

isting grant may be made as soon as notice is given. Rights under a renegotiated contract do not ripen until termination takes effect.

A notice of termination must contain certain basic information:

1. The name of the persons whose rights are being terminated and the address to which the notice is being sent. If you are sending notice to more than one address, list all of them.

2. The title of the work.

3. The name of at least one author of the work.

4. The date that copyright was secured.

5. The copyright registration number, if possible.

6. The exact nature of the grant you are terminating.

7. The date that termination is to become effective.

8. If the grant was made by someone other than the author, a list of all persons who made the original grant and who are still alive.

9. If the grant was made by the author, but is being terminated by his family, a list of all the persons who are entitled to take part in termination (whether they are actually doing so or not) and their relationships to the author. Indicate on the list which persons actually are taking part in the termination and what their percentage shares of the termination right are.

If you are not sure of all this information, put down as much as you know and explain why you are uncertain as to the rest.

The notice must be signed by all persons taking part. Each signature should be accompanied by the person's name and address, in legible form. The notice must also contain a statement that to the best of their knowledge those persons have among them a sufficiently large share of the termination right to entitle them to terminate.

The notice must be delivered by hand or by first-class mail. It is your duty to make reasonably sure that the person to whom you are giving the notice is still the owner of the right and has not granted it to someone else, and also that you have the correct address. This means that you should write to the Copyright Office and request a search for recordations of any transfers. (This will probably incur a small fee.) In the case of musical works, you should also check with the performing-rights societies, ASCAP, BMI, and SESAC.

If you fail to comply with any of these requirements and if your errors or omissions cause other people to be misled in some harmful way, your notice of termination may be judged legally ineffective.

Effect of These Rules on Derivative Works

Because expiration of copyright in an underlying work throws substantial portions of a derivative work into the public domain, it has been common practice for movie producers, for example, to make sure that copyright in the novels they use for their plots is renewed. This will continue to be valid practice.

Termination of a renewal term grant to make a derivative work will not prevent any such work already made from being exploited. For example, if a novelist terminates a grant to a film producer, that will only prevent the producer from making a new film of the same story, not from performing a film already made.

10 Tax Treatment of Copyrights

Authors generally have two tax problems: how to report their income and how to deduct their expenses. Other copyright owners have similar problems but from a different perspective. For them the problems are not much different from those of someone who buys a machine or farm. For an author, though, Congress has created a veritable funhouse of rules.

The Author as Owner: When Is an Asset Not an Asset?

The author's trouble arises principally from governmental ambivalence as to whether a copyright is a capital asset in the hands of its creator. In many respects an author is like someone who builds houses rather than like someone who buys them: his profit is taxed as ordinary income. Nonetheless, if he is a professional author he must treat some of his expenses as capital investments, and if he is not he must treat them all as capital investments. When and how those expenses can later be deducted also depends on whether the author is a professional.

As you can see, this is not an area where common sense or logic will necessarily be of help. The thing to have is a map and a rulebook, and I hope what follows will serve.

The Amateur

An amateur author cannot deduct any of the expenses of his hobby unless and until he sells the work.[1] An amateur author is one who is not engaged in the trade or business of creating copyrighted works. For example, someone who paints for recreation is an amateur for tax purposes, however good the paintings may be.

The question that decides whether someone is an amateur or a professional is whether the activity is carried on primarily for livelihood or profit or primarily for recreation. Dim hopes of future glory will not convert a hobby into a trade. On the other hand financial failure does not brand one as an amateur, if one has made a genuine effort to sell one's creations.[2] Nor is it necessary that the activity be one's sole pursuit in life: painting on weekends may still be a profession if you are actively trying to sell the results.

The regularity with which you pursue an activity will help determine whether you are a professional or an amateur.[3] The tortoise is more professional than the hare.

The Professional

Generally, if you are a professional author, costs relating to your title in a copyright cannot be deducted in the year you incur them. Instead they have to be capitalized—that is, treated as investments—and depreciated over the useful life of a copyright. Other expenses, such as travel, secretarial help, or supplies, may be deducted in the year they are incurred. The basic principles are these:

Costs Relating to Title

This phrase covers the cost of copyright registration, including legal fees. It also covers all expenses, including legal fees, you may incur in defending your copyright against someone who accuses you of infringing or in suing an infringer yourself. However, it does not include expenses incurred or damages won in defending or asserting a right to income. By the same token, damages that are in the form of profits are taxed as ordinary income. Damages that relate to title are not taxable as income but the amount of them must be subtracted from the capital basis on which you compute depreciation.

This is the sort of hairsplitting that has earned the Internal Revenue Code a bad name. Suppose you become involved in a complicated infringement suit, where not only the basic title to copyright but also the right to royalties is at stake. How do you decide where title ends and the right to royalties begins? The best you can do is to ask the court to apportion the damages it awards you between the two and apply the same ratio to your legal costs and to the damages you win. Sometimes your attorney will be able to give you an itemized bill, but this method of allocating legal costs runs a risk of being overruled by the IRS.

The foregoing applies only if you win. If the court decides your claimed copyright is invalid and you lose, all of your expenses will be deductible in the year the decision is handed down, and you will also be able to deduct the dollar value of the title you have lost (but not the value of projected income) in the year the decision is handed down. Expenses that arise from litigation over income will be deductible when paid.

Other Expenses   The deductibility of expenses incurred in creating a work is subject to complex rules. For a brief period Congress tried to subject all authors' expenses to the so-called uniform capitalization rules, so that all of these expenses would have to be capitalized rather than deducted. In response to an outcry from authors' groups, Congress quickly retreated, but left in place the following:

• In general no current deduction is allowed unless you are self-employed.

• Writers, composers, photographers, and artists are allowed to deduct most expenses in the year incurred, but it appears, somewhat ambiguously, that this is not allowed to filmmakers.

• Expenses relating to printing, photographic plates, motion picture films, videotapes, or similar items are not deductible but must be capitalized. Just what are "similar items" is unclear, but judging by the items listed one would have to extend this rule to, say, the costs a sculptor incurs in casting in bronze.

• No current deduction is allowed to an artist—as distinct from an author or photographer—unless the individual is "engaged in the business of being an artist." In this seemingly redundant provision a troublesome value judgment lurks: Congress does not regard anyone as an "artist" for tax purposes unless the aesthetic value of the work produced "predominates" over the utilitarian value. Thus, for example, says the legislative report accompanying the statute, "an expense that is incurred in producing jewelry, silverware, pottery, furniture, or other similar household items generally is not considered as being paid or incurred in the business of an individual being an artist." One can foresee much litigation from the crafts industry in challenging, or trying to narrow, this presumptuous generalization.

• Artists who do not qualify for current deduction treatment are given a "safe harbor"; they can deduct 50 percent of their expenses in the year incurred and 25 percent in each of the next two years.[4]

Depreciation   The tax laws permit an author to take a deduction each year for a portion of the capital value of a copyright, until it is reduced almost to zero. Depreciation should be taken over the useful life of the copyright. The presumption is that copyright will retain its value for its entire duration: life plus fifty years, or whatever the applicable term is. However, if you can prove that your copyright has a market life of only a few years, you can speed up your depreciation. Thus if you have written a textbook with a predictable market life of only six years, you can deduct one-sixth of your capital costs in each of those six years, starting with the year of first publication.[5] The general rule for depreciation is that it cannot begin until the asset is "placed in service." With works that are not published but are exploited by performance or display, depreciation would begin when exploitation begins. An interesting question, to which no one has the answer, is whether an unpublished work is "placed in service" when derivative works based upon it are published. I tend to think it should be so treated.

I use the phrase "almost to zero" because until you dispose of your copyright you cannot depreciate it below what is termed "salvage value."[6] Salvage value is, basically, what you could get for the copyright, even after income has dwindled away, by selling it to some optimistic buyer who hopes for a backswing in the pendulum of public taste or who wants to be able to use parts of your work without threat of suit. In most cases salvage value will be negligible. If your copyright is valuable, though, salvage may be a factor. You should consult your tax advisor on this point as on many of the other points noted here.

Matching Depreciation to Income   If you sell your copyright for a flat fee, you can deduct the remaining balance of your capital value in the year of sale. However, if you sell on a royalty basis, you should take your depreciation deductions against royalty income. In such a case the rules differ depending on whether you can predict your income flow. If you can, you should adjust your depreciation accordingly. For example, if you can predict that income will be $20,000 in the first year, $10,000 in the second year, $5,000 in the third, and zero in the fourth, for a total of $35,000, you can deduct twenty thirty-fifths of your capital value in the first year, ten thirty-fifths in the second, and the remaining five thirty-fifths in the third (always, of course, allowing for salvage value).[7] If you cannot predict your income flow, you can deduct for depreciation in any given year only up to the amount of income you receive.[8]

Deduction for Loss

If you abandon or forfeit your copyright, if it is taken away from you in a lawsuit, or if it becomes valueless, you can deduct the remaining balance of your capital value in the year the loss occurs.[9]

Special Problems for Sculpture, Paintings, and Plates

This discussion has so far dealt with the copyright itself, an intangible property right. A sculptor or painter, however, produces something tangible as well, quite apart from the copyright in the work. So does a printmaker or photographer. So too does a publisher.

The physical object has a value quite separate from that of the copyright. It is a capital-type asset. Because of this the costs of the materials and so on that go into it must be capitalized, even though they might otherwise be regarded as business expenses. Sometimes this will lead to allocation problems. For example, if you are a welder in steel, what part of your electricity costs has to be attributed to the object? Your guess is probably as good as the IRS's so long as you guess in good faith. Depreciation cannot be taken unless the object is likely to deteriorate noticeably in the owner's lifetime. Sale of the object by the author will produce ordinary income, against which the author can deduct any remaining capital basis.

Joint Authors

Where there are two or more joint authors, the depreciation basis must be divided among them in the same proportions as their ownership. Unless there is an agreement to the contrary, each joint author will take an equal share of the basis.

Gift and Estate Taxes

When an author makes a private gift of a copyright, it is valued for gift tax purposes not at its capital basis value but at its fair market value. It may have a basis of only $200, but if its market value (based on projected income) is $20,000, the author is treated as making a gift of $20,000. Yet, ironically a gift to charity will be valued not at fair market value but at the author's capital value.

Whether a gift other than to charity will actually incur gift tax depends on the number of donees, whether the author's spouse joins in making the gift, and whether the author has used up his "unified credit against gift and estate taxes." These are complex questions and outside the scope of this book. If you are making a gift to any one person of a copyright with a probable market value of over $10,000— the limit on tax-free gifts in any given year—you should consult a tax advisor.

A gift of a royalty interest will not circumvent this rule. Indeed, a gift of a royalty interest, without any transfer of ownership, will not even suffice to make the income taxable to the donee rather than the author, although it will nonetheless be taxed as a gift.[10]

This problem is frequently encountered by authors who wish to shift the future income stream of a work to their children, or to trusts for their children. The usual solution is to assign all copyright interests to the donee and, if the work is under contract for publication, to assign the *entire* contract, not merely the right to royalties.

Although unified with the gift tax laws in some respects, the estate tax laws as they apply to copyrights differ from the scheme I have described for gifts. A copyright is valued in the author's estate at its market value, no matter whether it is left to private persons or to charity. Thus if a copyright is left to charity—for example, as Shaw left his copyrights to the National Gallery of Ireland—the estate reports the full value in its inventory and receives as an offset a charitable deduction for the full value.

Special Rules for Corporations

Copyright in a film or other work produced by a large corporation, whose creative staff are paid a salary and have no financial stake in the corporation, in many cases will be treated as a capital asset if the corporation is in the trade or business of exploiting it rather than of selling or brokering it.[11]

Copyright as Capital Asset: Persons Other Than the Author

A different set of rules applies to a person to whom the author gives, bequeaths, or sells his copyright. The basis for such a person depends on which type of transfer occurs.

Basis in an Acquired Copyright

Donees

Basis in a gift is determined by looking at what lawyers call the owner's "chain of title." If you obtain a copyright by gift, your basis depends on who gave it to you. If you got it from the author, your basis is the author's basis, less any depreciation already taken before it reaches you. The same is true if you got it from someone who was given it by the author. There can be any number of gifts, but if the chain began with the author, the author's basis (as adjusted along the way) will be the basis for every owner in the chain. However, if someone in the chain of title purchased or inherited the copyright, the basis you get is that purchase price, or the estate value, less any depreciation taken on it since then. Each purchase or inheritance in a chain of title establishes a new basis for the copyright.

Inheritors

The tax laws give a break to someone who receives a copyright by inheritance. Basis is "stepped up" to the value of the copyright in the author's estate. Admittedly this makes a strange distinction between, say, a child of an author who is given a copyright and a child who gets it by inheritance. This distinction is sometimes overlooked by well-meaning parents; here, again, it is wise to seek the advice of a tax lawyer.

Purchasers

If you purchase a copyright, your basis will be what you paid for it. However, for there to have been a purchase, there has to have been a sale. The term *sale*, as used in the tax laws, has a special meaning. Because a copyright is a bundle of distinct rights, there can be a sale of one of those rights even if the others are retained. For example, you can have a sale of the publication right alone. However, if the transferor retains too much control over the right, there is no sale even though, for purposes of the copyright law, there has been an exclusive transfer.

The only controls that a seller can safely retain without running afoul of this rule are the right to sue for infringement and the right to rescind the transfer for failure to make royalty payments or because the

transferee has gone bankrupt, or because the transferee fails to market the property. The general principle here is that a transfer is a sale so long as
rescission can occur only because of some event that
is not in the seller's control.[12] The statutory right to
terminate a transfer (see chapters 3 and 9) does not
affect the status of a "sale."

A transfer may be limited in geographical scope. If
it is, it should be paid for not on a royalty basis but
in a lump sum, or it will be treated as a license and
not a sale. Conversely, if paid for on a royalty basis it
will be considered a sale only if the exclusive rights
given are without geographical limitation.[13] And all
of this is without regard to whether the arrangement
would be called a transfer of ownership for copyright
purposes.

In many cases, a purchaser will want to have a
transfer characterized as a license so that he can deduct his payments as a cost of doing business instead
of capitalizing them. The seller is just as likely to
want the opposite. When the transaction is ambiguous, this will be an important bargaining point for
both sides.

Depreciation   A donee or inheritor of a copyright can take depreciation only if a copyright is producing income. A purchaser of a copyright, assuming that the purchaser
has acquired the property for investment purposes
and not as a broker or trader in copyrights, can take
depreciation regardless of whether income is being
received. A broker or trader in copyrights holds the
copyrights as inventory and cannot take depreciation
at all.

The depreciation rules for someone who receives a
copyright by gift or inheritance are generally the
same as for an author: depreciation may be taken

against income in any of the ways discussed. A purchaser of a copyright must also follow these rules if he holds the copyright for investment purposes, except that he can take a deduction in a year of no income. All three types of persons can take a deduction for loss or forfeiture.

11

International Copyright Protection

If you know something of the life of Charles Dickens, you know something also of the chaos that existed in the early days of bulk printing, when, in the view of the U.S. Government, copyrights stopped at the borders of an author's native land. Dickens and other popular English writers suffered wholesale piracy of their works by American printers, until at last the U.S. Senate, against strong domestic pressure, agreed by treaty to recognize English copyrights.

Copyright is intrinsically a creature of national law. However, there are now few countries that do not have treaty arrangements for the international protection of copyrights. Most of these countries are members of either or both of the two great conventions, as they are called: the Berne Convention and the Universal Copyright Convention. These conventions are essentially multilateral agreements to give certain recognition to copyrights that arise in other member countries. Neither of these conventions requires a member nation to protect copyright in sound recordings. There is a separate treaty on this subject: the Convention for the Protection of Producers of Phonograms Against Unauthorized Duplication of Their Phonograms. However, the membership of this convention is comparatively small.

The United States was one of the founding members of the UCC in the early 1950s, but did not join Berne until 1989. The United States pushed for the formation of the UCC as an alternative to Berne; it declined for decades to join Berne out of a reluctance to abandon the notice requirement and certain other formalities and to extend copyright duration to meet Berne standards. It has finally succumbed, with the results I have described in preceding chapters.

Nearly every country in the world belongs to one of the two conventions; most belong to both. A few holdouts remain, such as the People's Republic of China, but the trend is toward wider membership, and through this and other methods copyright piracy has been substantially reduced. Most of our major trading partners belong to Berne. Even the Soviet Union, which did not join the UCC until 1973, has now announced that it will join Berne. If this pattern toward dual membership continues, eventually the UCC may die of irrelevance.[1]

Both Berne and the UCC live largely by two key precepts: "national treatment" and the setting of minimum standards of protection by which all treaty members must abide. National treatment requires that every member nation extend the protection of its laws to works that originate in other member nations. Thus an American sculptor must receive in Italy the same copyright treatment as an Italian sculptor, and the Italian must receive in the United States the same treatment as her American counterpart.

There are two qualifications to this. The first is the "rule of the shorter term," which is, in practice, more an exception than a rule. It permits the United States to protect foreign photographs, for example, only for as long as they would be protected in their countries of origin. To some this seems perverse, as denying Babe Ruth a homer to left in Wrigley Field if the ball wouldn't have cleared the wall at Fenway Park. To others it seems eminently fair; after all, if the author's own government doesn't care to protect him, why should the United States? However one views the rule, it is becoming less and less of an issue.

The United States has not taken much advantage of the rule, even though by a curious historical inversion this country now protects some copyrights—for example, in photographs—longer than many charter members of Berne. A few countries do exercise their right to apply the rule; given our present law on copyright duration, however, U.S. authors will generally not find this a barrier unless their works predate the 1976 Act.

Under Berne the rule of the shorter term can be applied on a case-by-case basis. Thus, for example, if an American film has gone into the public domain because of failure to renew, other countries will not be obliged to protect it thereafter. (Most will anyway.) Under the UCC the rule can be invoked only if the foreign work belongs to a *class* of works that receives shorter protection in the country of origin.[2]

The other qualification to national treatment favors developing countries. Both Berne and the UCC give these countries the right to reproduce foreign works for teaching purposes, on a sort of compulsory license basis, if no edition is generally available in those countries at a "reasonable price." Both also give some developing countries the right to publish unauthorized translations. The conditions that must be met for either of these rights to be invoked are complicated,[3] and I will not explicate them here. I will allow myself the observation that though the purpose of these provisions is laudable, the method seems unfair. Steel companies are not told that they must sell their steel at a discount to developing countries; if they do so, one government or the other subsidizes them. Why should copyright owners bear a different burden?

National treatment does not govern issues of ownership. If a work belongs to an employer as made-for-hire under U.S. law, it will not be treated otherwise by our Berne partners. Most countries do, however, impose their own rules on the validity of copyright transfers that allocate rights within their borders. For example, in Europe no license of rights in a joint work can be made except by all the joint authors. A French court will treat any license by only one author as invalid, to the extent it purports to give publication rights in France, even if the work is a U.S. work and the license is executed in the United States.[4]

The second key concept of Berne and the UCC is, as I mentioned, the setting of standards. Berne requires longer terms of protection than the UCC and eschews formalities; Berne is also more favorable to authors in the area of moral rights. The UCC, though it does not encourage formalities, does essentially codify pre-1976 U.S. law; it establishes "© [name] [year of first publication]" as a sort of international form of copyright notice. It is wise to use this UCC-approved form of notice to ensure protection in other UCC countries.

The trend, as I have said, is toward wider membership, enhanced standards of protection, greater uniformity of law, and less piracy. Overall we now operate in an international system that ensures American copyright owners reasonably predictable and uniform protection throughout most of the world. As international trade in copyrights becomes more and more valuable—in science, software, and entertainment—this system will likely prove to have been not merely fair-minded but foresighted as well.

Afterword

Information is power, as we are often told. But like most other kinds of power, it has no value except in use. We as a society benefit from that use and so we encourage authors as best we know how, realizing, as Samuel Johnson once put it, that "nobody but a blockhead ever wrote except for money."

However, as international copyright law demonstrates, people outside the free-market democracies do not view this equation in the same way. Our economies require raw materials; what the economies of developing countries require from us above all else—more than consumer goods and fancy weapons and the other vanities of modern life—is information. If they are to modernize, they must have access to our technical and scientific literature. In many cases these countries have agreed to pay for it only after receiving substantial concessions.

The international copyright system works reasonably well at the moment. But there are difficulties ahead. As computer software increases the sophistication of our technology, the gap that separates the haves from the have-nots will widen. Will the developing countries honor the claims of our authors in this field, or will they encourage the growth of a black market? This is one of many problems that will arise in applying copyright to computer software.

In 1909 when the predecessor to our current Copyright Act was passed, few if any foresaw the phenomenal development of radio, television, or sound recording. Yet these three media have radically changed our culture, and for many people they have greater importance than the printed word, which was once all-powerful. Few if any foresaw the advent of photocopying, which now poses such a threat to the publishing industry. In each case lawyers and their clients found themselves having to discuss new concepts in an old language. As Congress dickered and delayed, the courts were obliged to apply a sometimes outmoded statute as best they could. The results were uneven.

Now we have caught up, but one wonders for how long. Already computer technology is creating problems, and what new technologies may arise, many of you who read this book probably know far better than I.

I am not sure there is a solution to this problem. One way or another the copyright law has managed to adapt and survive. Some doctrines have been abandoned in the process; new ones have been acquired; others have scarcely changed in 200 years. There is a real virtue in this process, for it makes us focus on principles. Perhaps, as time goes on, we are developing a sense of what may be jettisoned in the cause of progress and what may not.

That has not been my main purpose in writing this book. My main purpose has been to acquaint you with the law as it is. However, if information really is power, what I have said may help you to contribute to the growth and orderly change of that law. That would be a benefit to all of us.

Appendix A

Methods of Affixation and Positions of the Copyright Notice on Various Types of Works [37 C.F.R. CH. II §201.20]

(a) *General.* (1) This section specifies examples of methods of affixation and positions of the copyright notice on various types of works that will satisfy the notice requirement of section 401(c) of title 17 of the United States Code, as amended by Pub. L. 94–553. A notice considered "acceptable" under this regulation shall be considered to satisfy the requirement of that section that it be "affixed to the copies in such manner and location as to give reasonable notice of the claim to copyright." As provided by that section, the examples specified in this regulation shall not be considered exhaustive of methods of affixation and positions giving reasonable notice of the claim of copyright.

(2) The provisions of this section are applicable to copies publicly distributed on or after December 1, 1981. This section does not establish any rules concerning the form of the notice or the legal sufficiency of particular notices, except with respect to methods of affixation and positions of notice. The adequacy or legal sufficiency of a copyright notice is determined

by the law in effect at the time of first publication of the work.

(b) *Definitions.* For the purposes of this section:

(1) The terms "audiovisual works," "collective works," "copies," "device," "fixed," "machine," "motion picture," "pictorial, graphic, and sculptural works," and their variant forms, have the meanings given to them in section 101 of title 17.

(2) "Title 17" means title 17 of the United States Code, as amended by Pub. L. 94–553.

(3) In the case of a work consisting preponderantly of leaves on which the work is printed or otherwise reproduced on both sides, a "page" is one side of a leaf; where the preponderance of the leaves are printed on one side only, the terms "page" and "leaf" mean the same.

(4) A work is published in "book form" if the copies embodying it consist of multiple leaves bound, fastened, or assembled in predetermined order as, for example, a volume, booklet, pamphlet, or multipage folder. For the purpose of this section, a work need not consist of textual matter in order to be considered published in "book form."

(5) A "title page" is a page, or two consecutive pages facing each other, appearing at or near the front of the copies of work published in book form, on which the complete title of the work is prominently stated and on which the names of the author or authors, the name of the publisher, the place of publication, or some combination of them, are given.

(6) The meaning of the terms "front," "back," "first," "last," and "following," when used in connection with works published in book form, will vary in relation to the physical form of the copies, depending on the particular language in which the work is written.

(7) In the case of a work published in book form with a hard or soft cover, the "front page" and "back page" of the copies are the outsides of the front and back covers; where there is no cover, the "front page" and "back page" are the pages visible at the front and back of the copies before they are opened.

(8) A "masthead" is a body of information appearing in approximately the same location in most issues of a newspaper, magazine, journal, review, or other periodical or serial, typically containing the title of the periodical or serial, information about the staff, periodicity of issues, operation, and subscription and editorial policies of the publication.

(9) A "single-leaf work" is a work published in copies consisting of a single leaf, including copies on which the work is printed or otherwise reproduced on either one side or on both sides of the leaf, and also folders which, without cutting or tearing the copies, can be opened out to form a single leaf. For the purpose of this section, a work need not consist of textual matter to be considered a "single-leaf work."

(c) *Manner of Affixation and Position Generally.* (1) In all cases dealt with in this section, the acceptability of a notice depends on its being permanently legible to an ordinary user of the work under normal conditions of use, and affixed to the copies in such manner and position that, when affixed, it is not concealed from view upon reasonable examination.

(2) Where, in a particular case, a notice does not appear in one of the precise locations prescribed in this section but a person looking in one of those locations would be reasonably certain to find a notice in another somewhat different location, that notice will be acceptable under this section.

(d) *Works Published in Book Form.* In the case of

works published in book form, a notice reproduced on the copies in any of the following positions is acceptable:

(1) The title page, if any.

(2) The page immediately following the title page, if any;

(3) Either side of the front cover, if any; or, if there is no front cover, either side of the front leaf of the copies;

(4) Either side of the back cover, if any; of, if there is no back cover, either side of the back leaf of the copies;

(5) The first page of the main body of the work;

(6) The last page of the main body of the work;

(7) Any page between the front page and the first page of the main body of the work; if: (i) There are no more than ten pages between the front page and the first page of the main body of the work; and (ii) the notice is reproduced prominently and is set apart from other matter on the page where it appears;

(8) Any page between the last page of the main body of the work and back page, if: (i) There are no more than ten pages between the last page of the main body of the work and the back page; and (ii) the notice is reproduced prominently and is set apart from the other matter on the page where it appears.

(9) In the case of a work published as an issue of a periodical or serial, in addition to any of the locations listed in paragraphs (d)(1) through (8) of this section, a notice is acceptable if it is located: (i) As a part of, or adjacent to, the masthead; (ii) on the page containing the masthead if the notice is reproduced prominently and is set apart from the other matter appearing on the page; or (iii) adjacent to a prominent heading, appearing at or near the front of the issue, containing the title of the periodical or serial

and any combination of the volume and issue number and date of the issue.

(10) In the case of musical work, in addition to any of the locations listed in paragraphs (d)(1) through (9) of this section, a notice is acceptable if it is located on the first page of music.

(e) *Single-Leaf Works.* In the case of single-leaf works, a notice reproduced on the copies anywhere on the front or back of the leaf is acceptable.

(f) *Contributions to Collective Works.* For a separate contribution to a collective work to be considered to "bear its own notice of copyright," as provided by 17 U.S.C. 404, a notice reproduced on the copies in any of the following positions is acceptable:

(1) Where the separate contribution is reproduced on a single page, a notice is acceptable if it appears: (i) Under the title of the contribution on that page; (ii) adjacent to the contribution; or (iii) on the same page if, through format, wording, or both, the application of the notice to the particular contribution is made clear;

(2) Where the separate contribution is reproduced on more than one page of the collective work, a notice is acceptable if it appears: (i) Under a title appearing at or near the beginning of the contribution; (ii) on the first page of the main body of the contribution; (iii) immediately following the end of the contribution; or (iv) on any of the pages where the contribution appears, if: (A) The contribution is reproduced on no more than twenty pages of the collective work; (B) the notice is reproduced prominently and is set apart from other matter on the page where it appears; and (C) through format, wording, or both, the application of the notice to the particular contribution is made clear;

(3) Where the separate contribution is a musical

work, in addition to any of the locations listed in paragraphs (f)(1) and (2) of this section, a notice is acceptable if it is located on the first page of music of the contribution;

(4) As an alternative to placing the notice on one of the pages where a separate contribution itself appears, the contribution is considered to "bear its own notice" if the notice appears clearly in juxtaposition with a separate listing of the contribution by title, or, if the contribution is untitled, by a description reasonably identifying the contribution: (i) on the page bearing the copyright notice for the collective work as a whole, if any; or (ii) in a clearly identified and readily-accessible table of contents or listing of acknowledgements appearing near the front or back of the collective work as a whole.

(g) *Works Reproduced in Machine-Readable Copies.* For works reproduced in machine-readable copies (such as magnetic tapes or disks, punched cards, or the like, from which the work cannot ordinarily be visually perceived except with the aid of a machine or device,[1] each of the following constitute examples of acceptable methods of affixation and position of notice:

(1) A notice embodied in the copies in machine-readable form in such a manner that on visually perceptible printouts it appears either with or near the title, or at the end of the work;

(2) A notice that is displayed at the user's terminal at sign on;

---

[1] Works published in a form requiring the use of a machine or device for purposes of optical enlargement (such as film, filmstrips, slide films, and works published in any variety of microform) and works published in visually perceptible form but used in connection with optical scanning devices, are not within this category.

(3) A notice that is continuously on terminal display;

(4) A legible notice reproduced durably, so as to withstand normal use, on a gummed or other label securely affixed to the copies or to a box, reel, cartridge, cassette, or other container used as a permanent receptacle for the copies.

(h) *Motion Pictures and Other Audiovisual Works.* (1) The following constitute examples of acceptable methods of affixation and positions of the copyright notice on motion pictures and other audiovisual works: A notice that is embodied in the copies by a photomechanical or electronic process, in such a position that it ordinarily would appear whenever the work is performed in its entirety, and that is located: (i) with or near the title; (ii) with the cast, credits, and similar information; (iii) at or immediately following the beginning of the work; or (iv) at or immediately preceding the end of the work.

(2) In the case of an untitled motion picture or other audiovisual work whose duration is sixty seconds or less, in addition to any of the locations listed in paragraph (h)(1) of this section, a notice that is embodied in the copies by a photomechanical or electronic process, in such a position that it ordinarily would appear to the projectionist or broadcaster when preparing the work for performance, is acceptable if it is located on the leader of the film or tape immediately preceding the beginning of the work.

(3) In the case of a motion picture or other audiovisual work that is distributed to the public for private use, the notice may be affixed, in addition to the locations specified in paragraph (h)(1) of this section, on the housing or container, if it is a permanent receptacle for the work.

(i) *Pictorial, Graphic, and Sculptural Works.* The following constitute examples of acceptable methods of affixation and positions of the copyright notice on various forms of pictorial, graphic, and sculptural works:

(1) Where a work is reproduced in two-dimensional copies, a notice affixed directly or by means of a label cemented, sewn, or otherwise attached durably, so as to withstand normal use, to the front or back of the copies, or to any backing, mounting, matting, framing, or other material to which the copies are durably attached, so as to withstand normal use, or in which they are permanently housed, is acceptable.

(2) Where a work is reproduced in three-dimensional copies, a notice affixed directly or by means of a label cemented, sewn, or otherwise attached durably, so as to withstand normal use, to any visible portion of the work, or to any base, mounting, framing, or other material on which the copies are durably attached, so as to withstand normal use, or in which they are permanently housed, is acceptable.

(3) Where, because of the size or physical characteristics of the material in which the work is reproduced in copies, it is impossible or extremely impracticable to affix a notice to the copies directly or by means of a durable label, a notice is acceptable if it appears on a tag that is of durable material, so as to withstand normal use, and that is attached to the copy with sufficient durability that it will remain with the copy while it is passing through its normal channels of commerce.

(4) Where a work is reproduced in copies consisting of sheet-like or strip material bearing multiple or continuous reproductions of the work, the notice may be applied: (i) To the reproduction itself; (ii) to the margin, selvage, or reverse side of the material at

frequent and regular intervals; or (iii) if the material contains neither a selvage nor a reverse side, to tags and labels, attached to the copies and to any spools, reels, or containers housing them in such a way that a notice is visible while the copies are passing through their normal channels of commerce.

(5) If the work is permanently housed in a container, such as a game or puzzle box, a notice reproduced on the permanent container is acceptable.

Appendix B

FORM TX
UNITED STATES COPYRIGHT OFFICE

REGISTRATION NUMBER

	TX	TXU

EFFECTIVE DATE OF REGISTRATION

Month	Day	Year

DO NOT WRITE ABOVE THIS LINE. IF YOU NEED MORE SPACE, USE A SEPARATE CONTINUATION SHEET.

1

TITLE OF THIS WORK ▼

Touring Sunny Grenada

PREVIOUS OR ALTERNATIVE TITLES ▼

Hot Spot in the Caribbean   (alternative title)

PUBLICATION AS A CONTRIBUTION If this work was published as a contribution to a periodical, serial, or collection, give information about the collective work in which the contribution appeared. **Title of Collective Work ▼**

U.S. Marine Journal

If published in a periodical or serial give: **Volume ▼**	**Number ▼**	**Issue Date ▼**	**On Pages ▼**
15	4	11/1/83	15-24

2

NAME OF AUTHOR ▼

a   Roberta MacFarlane

DATES OF BIRTH AND DEATH
Year Born ▼ 1941   Year Died ▼

Was this contribution to the work a "work made for hire"?	AUTHOR'S NATIONALITY OR DOMICILE Name of Country	WAS THIS AUTHOR'S CONTRIBUTION TO THE WORK
☐ Yes ☒ No	OR { Citizen of ▶ U.S.A. Domiciled in ▶	Anonymous? ☐ Yes ☒ No Pseudonymous? ☐ Yes ☒ No If the answer to either of these questions is Yes, see detailed instructions

NATURE OF AUTHORSHIP Briefly describe nature of the material created by this author in which copyright is claimed. ▼
Text

NOTE

Under the law, the "author" of a "work made for hire" is generally the employer, not the employee (see instructions). For any part of this work that was "made for hire" check "Yes" in the space provided, give the employer (or other person for whom the work was prepared) as "Author" of that part, and leave the space for dates of birth and death blank.

NAME OF AUTHOR ▼

b   Georgina Schultz

DATES OF BIRTH AND DEATH
Year Born ▼ 1929   Year Died ▼

Was this contribution to the work a "work made for hire"?	AUTHOR'S NATIONALITY OR DOMICILE Name of country	WAS THIS AUTHOR'S CONTRIBUTION TO THE WORK
☐ Yes ☒ No	OR { Citizen of ▶ U.S.A. Domiciled in ▶	Anonymous? ☐ Yes ☒ No Pseudonymous? ☐ Yes ☒ No If the answer to either of these questions is Yes, see detailed instructions

NATURE OF AUTHORSHIP Briefly describe nature of the material created by this author in which copyright is claimed. ▼
Photographic illustrations

NAME OF AUTHOR ▼

c

DATES OF BIRTH AND DEATH
Year Born ▼   Year Died ▼

Was this contribution to the work a "work made for hire"?	AUTHOR'S NATIONALITY OR DOMICILE Name of Country	WAS THIS AUTHOR'S CONTRIBUTION TO THE WORK
☐ Yes ☐ No	OR { Citizen of ▶ Domiciled in ▶	Anonymous? ☐ Yes ☐ No Pseudonymous? ☐ Yes ☐ No If the answer to either of these questions is Yes, see detailed instructions

NATURE OF AUTHORSHIP Briefly describe nature of the material created by this author in which copyright is claimed. ▼

3

YEAR IN WHICH CREATION OF THIS WORK WAS COMPLETED This information must be given in all cases.	DATE AND NATION OF FIRST PUBLICATION OF THIS PARTICULAR WORK Complete this information ONLY if this work has been published.
1983 ◀ Year	Month ▶ November Day ▶ 01 Year ▶ 83 U.S.A. ◀ Nation

4

COPYRIGHT CLAIMANT(S) Name and address must be given even if the claimant is the same as the author given in space 2. ▼

Carribee Publishers, Inc.
54 Manitou Drive
Conch Shell, Florida 33904

See instructions before completing this space.

TRANSFER If the claimant(s) named here in space 4 are different from the author(s) named in space 2, give a brief statement of how the claimant(s) obtained ownership of the copyright. ▼

Written transfer of all right, title, and interest.

APPLICATION RECEIVED

ONE DEPOSIT RECEIVED

TWO DEPOSITS RECEIVED

REMITTANCE NUMBER AND DATE

DO NOT WRITE HERE — OFFICE USE ONLY

MORE ON BACK ▶ • Complete all applicable spaces (numbers 5-11) on the reverse side of this page.   • See detailed instructions.   • Sign the form at line 10.

DO NOT WRITE HERE

Page 1 of _____ pages

EXAMINED BY		FORM TX
CHECKED BY		
☐ CORRESPONDENCE Yes		FOR COPYRIGHT OFFICE USE ONLY
☐ DEPOSIT ACCOUNT FUNDS USED		

DO NOT WRITE ABOVE THIS LINE. IF YOU NEED MORE SPACE, USE A SEPARATE CONTINUATION SHEET.

PREVIOUS REGISTRATION Has registration for this work, or for an earlier version of this work, already been made in the Copyright Office?
☒ Yes ☐ No If your answer is "Yes," why is another registration being sought? (Check appropriate box) ▼
☐ This is the first published edition of a work previously registered in unpublished form.
☐ This is the first application submitted by this author as copyright claimant.
☒ This is a changed version of the work, as shown by space 6 on this application.
If your answer is "Yes," give: **Previous Registration Number ▼**   **Year of Registration ▼**
     TX 1 – 156 – 780   1982

(5)

DERIVATIVE WORK OR COMPILATION Complete both space 6a & 6b for a derivative work; complete only 6b for a compilation.
a. Preexisting Material Identify any preexisting work or works that this work is based on or incorporates ▼
    Castro's Third World Colonies (an article in U.S. Marine Journal, vol. 14, no. 1)

b. Material Added to This Work Give a brief, general statement of the material that has been added to this work and in which copyright is claimed. ▼
    Text has been substantially revised, and photographs are all new.

See instructions before completing this space

(6)

MANUFACTURERS AND LOCATIONS If this is a published work consisting preponderantly of nondramatic literary material in English, the law may require that the copies be manufactured in the United States or Canada for full protection. If so, the names of the manufacturers who performed certain processes, and the places where these processes were performed **must be given.** See instructions for details.
Names of Manufacturers ▼   **Places of Manufacture ▼**
   Typesetter: Tinker Text, Inc.   Potowatamee, Wisconsin
   Printer/Binder: Tailer Publishers   Oshkosh, Wisconsin

(7)

REPRODUCTION FOR USE OF BLIND OR PHYSICALLY HANDICAPPED INDIVIDUALS A signature on this form at space 10, and a check in one of the boxes here in space 8, constitutes a non-exclusive grant of permission to the Library of Congress to reproduce and distribute solely for the blind and physically handicapped and under the conditions and limitations prescribed by the regulations of the Copyright Office: (1) copies of the work identified in space 1 of this application in Braille (or similar tactile symbols); or (2) phonorecords embodying a fixation of a reading of that work; or (3) both.
   a ☒ Copies and Phonorecords   b ☐ Copies Only   c ☐ Phonorecords Only

See instructions

(8)

DEPOSIT ACCOUNT If the registration fee is to be charged to a Deposit Account established in the Copyright Office, give name and number of Account.
Name ▼   **Account Number ▼**

(9)

CORRESPONDENCE Give name and address to which correspondence about this application should be sent. Name/Address/Apt/City/State/Zip ▼
   Ephraim Lawless, Esq.
   Lawless & Wylde, P.C.
   200 State Street, Conch Shell, Florida 33904
      Area Code & Telephone Number ▶

Be sure to give your daytime phone ◀ number

CERTIFICATION* I, the undersigned, hereby certify that I am the
     ☐ author
     ☐ other copyright claimant
  Check one ▶ ☐ owner of exclusive right(s)
of the work identified in this application and that the statements made   ☒ authorized agent of Carribee Publishers, Inc.
by me in this application are correct to the best of my knowledge.   Name of author or other copyright claimant, or owner of exclusive right(s) ▲

Typed or printed name and date ▼ If this is a published work, this date must be the same as or later than the date of publication given in space 3.
   Manuel Hidalgo, President   **date ▶**

☞ **Handwritten signature (X) ▼**

(10)

MAIL CERTIFICATE TO	Name ▼
	Ephraim Lawless, Esq.
Certificate will be mailed in window envelope	Number/Street/Apartment Number ▼ Lawless & Wylde, P.C. 200 State Street
	City/State/ZIP ▼ Conch Shell, Florida 33904

Have you:
• Completed all necessary spaces?
• Signed your application in space 10?
• Enclosed check or money order for $10 payable to Register of Copyrights?
• Enclosed your deposit material with the application and fee?
MAIL TO: Register of Copyrights, Library of Congress, Washington, D.C. 20559

(11)

* 17 U.S.C. § 506(e) Any person who knowingly makes a false representation of a material fact in the application for copyright registration provided for by section 409, or in any written statement filed in connection with the application, shall be fined not more than $2,500.

⋆ U.S. GOVERNMENT PRINTING OFFICE: 1983: 381-278/503   August 1983—300,000

Circular R7b

"Best Edition" of Published Copyrighted Works for the Collections of the Library of Congress*

The Copyright Law (Title 17, United States Code) requires that copies or phonorecords deposited in the Copyright Office be of the "best edition" of the work. The law states that "The 'best edition' of a work is the edition, published in the United States at any time before the date of deposit, that the Library of Congress determines to be most suitable for its purposes."

When two or more editions of the same version of a work have been published, the one of the highest quality is generally considered to be the best edition. In judging quality, the Library of Congress will adhere to the criteria set forth below in all but exceptional circumstances.

Where differences between editions represent variations in copyrightable content, each edition is a separate version and "best edition" standards based on such differences do not apply. Each such version is a separate work for the purposes of the Copyright Law.

Appearing below are lists of criteria to be applied in determining the best edition of each of several types of material. The criteria are listed in descending order of importance. In deciding between two editions, a criterion-by-criterion comparison should be made. The edition which first fails to satisfy a criterion is to be considered of inferior quality and will not be an acceptable deposit. For example, if a comparison is made between two hardbound editions of a book, one a trade edition printed on acid-free paper and the other a specially bound edition printed on average paper, the former will be the best edition because the type of paper is a more important criterion than the binding.

Under regulations of the Copyright Office, potential depositors may request authorization to deposit copies or phonorecords of other than the best edition of a specific work (e.g., a microform rather than a printed edition of a serial).

I. PRINTED TEXTUAL MATTER

A. *Paper, Binding, and Packaging:*

1. Archival-quality rather than less-permanent paper.

2. Hard cover rather than soft cover.

3. Library binding rather than commercial binding.

4. Trade edition rather than book club edition.

5. Sewn rather than glue-only binding.

6. Sewn or glued rather than stapled or spiral-bound.

7. Stapled rather than spiral-bound or plastic-bound.

*This excerpt is taken from Volume 43, No. 2 of the *Federal Register* for Wednesday, January 4, 1978 (p. 766)

8. Bound rather than looseleaf, except when future looseleaf insertions are to be issued.

9. Slipcased rather than nonslipcased.

10. With protective folders rather than without (for broadsides).

11. Rolled rather than folded (for broadsides).

12. With protective coatings rather than without (except broadsides, which should not be coated).

B. *Rarity:*

1. Special limited edition having the greatest number of special features.
2. Other limited edition rather than trade edition.
3. Special binding rather than trade binding.

C. *Illustrations:*

1. Illustrated rather than unillustrated.
2. Illustrations in color rather than black and white.

D. *Special Features:*

1. With thumb notches or index tabs rather than without.
2. With aids to use such as overlays and magnifiers rather than without.

E. *Size:*

1. Larger rather than smaller sizes. (Except that large-type editions for the partially-sighted are not required in place of editions employing type of more conventional size.)

II. PHOTOGRAPHS

A. Size and finish, in descending order of preference:
1. The most widely distributed edition.
2. 8 × 10-inch glossy print.
3. Other size or finish.

B. Unmounted rather than mounted.

C. Archival-quality rather than less-permanent paper stock or printing process.

III. MOTION PICTURES

A. Film rather than another medium. Film editions are listed below in descending order of preference.
1. Preprint material, by special arrangement.
2. Film gauge in which most widely distributed.
3. 35 mm rather than 16 mm.
4. 16 mm rather than 8 mm.
5. Special formats (e.g., 65 mm) only in exceptional cases.
6. Open reel rather than cartridge or cassette.

B. Videotape rather than videodisc. Videotape editions are listed below in descending order of preference.
1. Tape gauge in which most widely distributed.
2. Two-inch tape.
3. One-inch tape.
4. Three-quarter-inch tape cassette.
5. One-half-inch tape cassette.

IV. OTHER GRAPHIC MATTER

A. *Paper and Printing:*
1. Archival quality rather than less-permanent paper.
2. Color rather than black and white.

B. *Size and Content:*
1. Larger rather than smaller size.
2. In the case of cartographic works, editions with the greatest amount of information rather than those with less detail.

C. *Rarity:*
1. The most widely distributed edition rather than one of limited distribution.
2. In the case of a work published only in a limited, numbered edition, one copy outside the numbered series but otherwise identical.
3. A photographic reproduction of the original, by special arrangement only.

D. *Text and Other Materials:*
1. Works with annotations, accompanying tabular or textual matter, or other interpretative aids rather than those without them.

E. *Binding and Packaging:*
1. Bound rather than unbound.
2. If editions have different binding, apply the criteria in I.A.2–I.A.7, above.
4. Rolled rather than folded.
5. With protective coatings rather than without.

V. PHONORECORDS

A. Disc rather than tape.

B. With special enclosures rather than without.

C. Open-reel rather than cartridge.

D. Cartridge rather than cassette.

E. Quadraphonic rather than stereophonic.

F. True stereophonic rather than monaural.

G. Monaural rather than electronically rechanneled stereo.

VI. MUSICAL COMPOSITIONS

A. *Fullness of Score:*
1. *Vocal music:*
  a. With orchestral accompaniment—
  i. Full score and parts, if any, rather than conductor's score and parts, if any. (In cases of compositions published only by rental, lease, or lending, this requirement is reduced to full score only.)
  ii. Conductor's score and parts, if any, rather than condensed score and parts, if any. (In cases of compo-

sitions published only by rental, lease, or lending, this requirement is reduced to conductor's score only.)
  b. Unaccompanied: Open score (each part on separate staff) rather than closed score (all parts condensed to two staves).
2. *Instrumental music:*
  a. Full score and parts, if any, rather than conductor's score and parts, if any. (In cases of compositions published only by rental, lease, or lending, this requirement is reduced to full score only.)
  b. Conductor's score and parts, if any, rather than condensed score and parts, if any. (In cases of compositions published only by rental, lease, or lending, this requirement is reduced to conductor's score only.)

B. *Printing and Paper:*
1. Archival-quality rather than less-permanent paper.

C. *Binding and Packaging:*
1. Special limited editions rather than trade editions.
2. Bound rather than unbound.
3. If editions have different binding, apply the criteria in I.A.2–I.A.12, above.
4. With protective folders rather than without.

VII. MICROFORMS

A. *Related Materials:*
1. With indexes, study guides, or other printed matter rather than without.

B. *Permanence and Appearance:*
1. Silver halide rather than any other emulsion.
2. Positive rather than negative.
3. Color rather than black and white.

C. *Format (newspapers and newspaper-formatted serials):*
1. Reel microfilm rather than any other microform.

D. *Format (all other materials):*
1. Microfiche rather than reel microfilm.
2. Reel microfilm rather than microform cassettes.
3. Microfilm cassettes rather than micro-opaque prints.

E. *Size:*
1. 35 mm rather than 16 mm.

VIII. WORKS EXISTING IN MORE THAN ONE MEDIUM

Editions are listed below in descending order of preference.

A. Newspapers, dissertations and theses, newspaper-formatted serials:
1. Microform.
2. Printed matter.

B. All other materials:
1. Printed matter.
2. Microform.
3. Phonorecord.
(Effective: January 1, 1978.)

For further information on Copyright Office deposit regulations, see Part 202 of 37 CFR, Chapter II, or write to the Register of Copyrights, Library of Congress, Washington, D.C. 20559.

Appendix D

Registration of Computer Programs and Databases

If you are considering registering copyright in an unpublished program or database that is fixed only in object form (what the regulations call "machine-readable form"), or in a published program or database that is published only in object form, the regulations call for the deposit of identifying material instead of a copy of the object code.

Computer Programs

1. In the case of a program, the general rule is to deposit the first 25 pages or equivalent units and the last 25 pages or equivalent units, in visually perceptible form, along with, if the work is published, the page or other unit containing the copyright notice (if any). "Visually perceptible form" means on paper or microform.

2. If you are registering a program and refer specifically to the scen displays on the application, you should deposit identifying material for those screen displays as well. Where authorship in the program is primarily literary, this may consist of print-outs, photographs, or drawings, which must be less than 3×3 inches and not greater than 9×12 inches in dimension. Where the authorship is primarily audio-

visual, the proper identifying material may instead be a ½-inch VHS videotape of the screen display sequence, provided this records what is actually fixed in the program and not what the user creates. The Copyright Office will not accept a videotape that is essentially a demonstration of how the program works. In no case will the Copyright Office accept a user manual as identifying material.

This distinction between "predominantly literary" and "predominantly audiovisual" is somewhat misleading. A video game clearly falls in the latter camp, and a complicated signal processing system in the former. But in between is a grey area of large dimensions. What of a computer-aided design program with a heavy visual component but no sound? It would probably be placed in the "literary" camp by default. The true distinction here is that only screen displays that are audiovisual works qualify for videotape deposit.

3. If the program you are depositing is a revision of a preexisting program, the deposit must be representative of the revisions that have been made. If the first 25 and the last 25 pages are not, then you should deposit any 50 representative pages.

4. If the program you are registering contains trade secret information—as most do—you can take advantage of certain special exceptions:

a. You can block out the trade secret portions, so long as the blocked out portions are "proportionally less" than what remains and an "appreciable amount of original computer code" is visible.

b. You can deposit the first 10 and last 10 pages with nothing blocked out.

c. You can deposit the first 25 and last 25 pages, with portions blocked out, plus 10 pages with nothing blocked out. If the program is a revised version, and the first 25 and last 25 pages are not representative of the new material, you can deposit 20 pages with nothing blocked out or 50 pages with block-outs, so long as in either case the pages are representative and, if you use block-outs, the material that remains is proportionately more than what you have blocked out and contains an appreciable amount of original code.

5. It should be noted that if the above strategies are undesirable for some good reason, you can apply to the Copyright Office for "special relief," in other words, a special dispensation from these requirements.

6. As an alternative to the above methods in trade secret situations, you can make your deposit in object code form only. The problem with this is that your registration is then made under the "rule of doubt." This means that the Copyright Office, in granting registration, is expressing no opinion on whether the object code actually embodies the work being registered. The registration is thus more open to attack than one for which identifying material has been deposited.

Databases

The deposit requirements for automated databases (those that are available in CD-ROM, on-line, or other electronic format) are these:

1. For a database on any single subject, the first 25 and last 25 pages or equivalent units, in visually perceptible form, are sufficient. Where the work is a revised version, the rule requires 50 pages that are representative of the revisions made.

2. For a database made up of data files covering two or more separate and distinct subjects, either fifty complete data records from each file or the entire file, whichever is less, in visually perceptible form. A

"data file" for these purposes is any group of data records, regardless of their size, that pertain to a common subject matter. You must also submit a descriptive statement, typed or printed, containing this information:

• the title of the database;

• a subtitle, date of creation or publication, or other information that will distinguish any separate or distinct data file for cataloguing purposes;

• the name and address of the copyright claimant;

• the name and content of each separate file, including subject matter, origin of the data (if the file is a revised version), and the approximate number of records in the file;

• if the work is published, an exact description of the copyright notice (if any) that is put on the work and the manner or frequency with which it is displayed—for example, at the user's terminal only at sign-on, or on printouts, or whatever.

A new procedure has been made available for registration of so-called dynamic databases—those that are updated frequently. The procedure permits registration of all revisions to the database that occur over any three consecutive months in one calendar year, for a single fee and using a single TX form. Special instructions are available from the Copyright Office for the completion of the form; they are complicated and some staff at the Copyright Office believe that in the end a new form will need to be developed. Do not hesitate to call the Office for help in any instance.

Group registration is available only if all of the updates and other revisions are owned by the same copyright claimant, have the same general title, and are similar in subject, content, and organization.

Deposit for a group registration must include 50

pages or equivalent units, or 50 data records, that are representative as of any one date of publication (or if the database is considered unpublished, as is often the case with on-line databases, one data of fixation). They must also be representative of the revisions generally and must either contain nothing but new material or be marked to show the new material added.

The statement accompanying deposit for a group registration must include, in addition to the usual information required for databases, a description of the nature and frequency of changes to the database, and it must identify at least in a general way the location within the database or the separate data files where the revisions are to be found.

Note that the representative date you choose for the deposit is also the date you must list as the publication date, in the case of a published database.

3. For any sort of database, if you affix a visually perceptible notice to the work or to the container in which you publish it, you should include a sample of that notice with your deposit. This is mandatory for registrations of multifile databases and for group registrations and is strongly advised, if not actually mandatory, for all others.

The rules discussed in this appendix are set out in 37 C.F.R. §202.20, as amended at 54 Fed. Reg. 13,173-13, 182 (March 31, 1989).

Appendix E

Warnings of Copyright for Use by Certain Libraries and Archives [37 C.F.R. Ch. II §201.14]

(a) *Definitions.* (1) A "Display Warning of Copyright" is a notice under paragraphs (d) (2) and (e) (2) of section 108 of Title 17 of the United States Code as amended by Pub. L. 94-553. As required by those sections the "Display Warning of Copyright" is to be displayed at the place where orders for copies or phonorecords are accepted at certain libraries and archives.

(2) An "Order Warning of Copyright" is a notice under paragraphs (d) (2) and (e) (2) of section 108 of Title 17 of the United States Code as amended by Pub. L. 94-553. As required by those sections the "Order Warning of Copyright" is to be included on printed forms supplied by certain libraries and archives and used by their patrons for ordering copies or phonorecords.

(b) *Contents.* A Display Warning of Copyright and an Order Warning of Copyright shall consist of a verbatim reproduction of the following notice, printed in such size and form and displayed in such manner as to comply with paragraph (c) of this section:

NOTICE

WARNING CONCERNING COPYRIGHT RESTRICTIONS

The copyright law of the United States (Title 17, United States Code) governs the making of photocopies or other reproductions of copyrighted material.

Under certain conditions specified in the law, libraries and archives are authorized to furnish a photocopy or other reproduction. One of these specified conditions is that the photocopy or reproduction is not to be "used for any purpose other than private study, scholarship, or research." If a user makes a request for, or later uses, a photocopy or a reproduction for purposes in excess of "fair use," that user may be liable for copyright infringement.

This institution reserves the right to refuse to accept a copying order if, in its judgment, fulfillment of the order would involve violation of copyright law.

(c) *Form and Manner of Use.* (1) A Display Warning of Copyright shall be printed on heavy paper or other durable material in type at least 18 points in size, and shall be displayed prominently, in such manner and location as to be clearly visible, legible, and comprehensible to a casual observer within the immediate vicinity of the place where orders are accepted.

(2) An Order Warning of Copyright shall be printed within a box located prominently on the order form itself, either on the front side of the form or immediately adjacent to the space calling for the name or signature of the person using the form. The notice shall be printed in type size no smaller than that used predominantly throughout the form, and in no case shall the type size be smaller than 8 points. The notice shall be printed in such manner as to be clearly legible, comprehensible, and readily apparent to a casual reader of the form.

Notes

Chapter 1

1. 17 U.S.C. §102(a).

2. 17 U.S.C. §301.

3. *See, e.g.*, Hoehling v. Universal City Studios, Inc., 618 F.2d 972 (2d Cir. 1980), *cert. denied* 449 U.S. 841 (1980); Miller v. Universal City Studios, Inc., 650 F.2d 1365 (5th Cir. 1981).

4. Sheldon v. Metro-Goldwyn Pictures Corp., 81 F.2d 49, 54 (2d Cir. 1936).

5. 17 U.S.C. §101.

6. Alfred Bell & Co. v. Catalda Fine Arts, Inc., 191 F.2d 99 (2d Cir. 1951), *aff'g* 74 F. Supp. 973 (S.D.N.Y. 1947); Alva Studios, Inc. v. Winninger, 177 F. Supp. 265 (S.D.N.Y. 1959). A recent case has held that affixing an art print to a ceramic tile creates a derivative work, but this is almost certainly an aberration. Mirage Editions, Inc. v. Albuquerque A.R.T. Co., 856 F.2d 1341 (9th Cir. 1988).

7. 17 U.S.C. § 103(b).

8. L. Batlin & Son, Inc. v. Snyder, 536 F.2d 436 (2d Cir. 1976); Durham Industries, Inc. v. Tomy Corp., 630 F.2d 905 (2d Cir. 1980); Gracen v Bradford Exchange, 698 F.2d 300 (7th Cir. 1983); Sunset House Distrib. Corp. v. Doran, 304 F.2d 251 (9th Cir. 1962),

aff'g 197 F. Supp. 940 (S.D.Cal. 1961). *See also* Knickerbocker Toy Co., Inc., v. Winterbrook Toy Corp., 216 U.S.P.Q. 621 (D.N.H. 1982).

9. A lucid and interesting discussion of this problem may be found in Oppenheimer, "Originality in Art Reproductions: 'Variations' in Search of a Theme," *Bull. Copr. Society* vol. 26, no. 1, 1978.

10. *See, e.g.,* Eckes v. Card Price Update, 736 F.2d 859 (2d Cir. 1984); *compare* Official Aviation Guide Co. v. American Aviation Associates, 150 F.2d 173 (7th Cir. 1945); Leon v. Pacific Tel. & Tel. Co., 91 F. 2d 484 (9th Cir. 1937); R. R. Donnelley & Sons Co. v. Haber, 43 F. Supp. 456 (E.D.N.Y. 1942); Jeweler's Circular Pub. Co. v. Keystone Publ. Co., 281 Fed. 83 (2d Cir. 1922).

11. Sometimes these rules are taken too far, as in Leon v. Pacific Tel. & Tel. Co., *supra; see* Triangle Publications, Inc. v. Sports Eye, Inc., 415 F. Supp. 682 (E.D.Pa. 1976).

12. *Compare* National Business Lists, Inc. v. Dun & Bradstreet, Inc., 215 U.S.P.Q. 595 (N.D.Ill. 1982) with New York Times Co. v. Roxbury Data Interface, Inc., 434 F. Supp. 217 (S.D.N.Y. 1977).

13. Gilliam v. American Broadcasting Companies, Inc., 538 F.2d 14 (2d Cir. 1976).

14. 101 U.S. 99 (1880).

15. Harcourt, Brace & World Inc. v. Graphic Controls Corp., 329 F. Supp. 517 (S.D.N.Y. 1971); Manpower, Inc. v. Temporary Help of Harrisburg, Inc., 246 F.Supp. 788 (E.D.Pa. 1865).

16. Morrissey v. Procter & Gamble Co., 379 F.2d 675 (1st Cir. 1967).

17. 17 U.S.C. §102(a).

18. Leon v. Pacific Tel. & Tel., *supra;* Amsterdam v.

Triangle Publications, Inc., 189 F.2d 104 (3rd Cir. 1951).

19. *See, e.g.*, Metropolitan Opera Association, Inc. v. Wagner-Nichols Recorder Corp., 199 Misc. 786, 101 N.Y.S.2d 483 (1950), *aff'd*, 279 App. Div. 632, 107 N.Y.S.2d 795 (1951).

20. Midler v. Ford Motor Co., 849 F.2d 460 (9th Cir. 1988). *See* Lennon v. Pulsebeat News, Inc., 143 U.S.P.Q. 309 (N.Y.Sup.Ct. 1964); Sinatra v. Goodyear Tire & Rubber Co., 435 F.2d 711 (9th Cir. 1979); Booth v. Colgate-Palmolive Co., 362 F.Supp. 343 (S.D.N.Y. 1973).

21. *See, e.g.*, Becker v. Loew's, Inc., 133 F.2d 889 (7th Cir. 1943); *compare* John Muller & Co. v. New York Arrows Soccer Team, Inc., 231 U.S.P.Q. 319 (8th Cir. 1986), with Reader's Digest Association, Inc. v. Conservative Digest, Inc., 821 F.2d 800 (D.C. Cir. 1987).

22. Paramore v. Mack Sennett, 9 F.2d 66 (S.D.Cal. 1925); *cf.* Duff v. Kansas City Star Co., 229 F.2d 320 (8th Cir. 1962). The scope of the law on unfair competition has been severely limited in recent years. Federal copyright law now preempts state laws in the field, to the extent they purport to protect rights equivalent to rights under copyright in works fixed in tangible form, whether or not they are copyrightable. 17 U.S.C. §301; H.R. Rep. No. 94-1476, 94th Cong., 2d Sess. 130–133 (1976). (This, the House of Representatives Report for the Copyright Act of 1976, will be referred to hereafter as "H. Rep.") This does not apply quite so broadly to causes of action arising before 1978. There is no reason to feel it would restrict protection of titles, because titles are regarded as trademarks under federal law, not as works of authorship.

23. H. Rep., pp. 53–54.

24. H. Rep., p. 55.

25. Brandir International, Inc. v. Cascade Pacific Lumber Co., 834 F.2d 1142 (2d Cir. 1987).

26. *Ibid.*; 17 U.S.C. §§101, 113(b); H. Rep., p. 105.

27. *Ibid.*; *see also, e.g.,* Muller v. Triborough Bridge Authority, 43 F. Supp. 298 (S.D.N.Y. 1974); DeSilva Construction Corp. v. Herrald, 213 F.Supp. 184 (N.D.Fla. 1962); Imperial Homes Corp. v. Lamont, 458 F.2. 895 (5th Cir. 1972); *but see* Herman Frankel Organization v. Wolfe, 184 U.S.P.Q. 819 (E.D.Mich. 1974). *Cf.* 17 U.S.C. §106(2), and *e.g.,* King Features Syndicate v. Fleischer, 299 Fed. 533 (2d Cir. 1924).

28. H. Rep., p. 55.

29. *Ibid.*

30. *See, e.g.,* Nichols v. Universal Pictures Corp., 45 F.2d 119 (1930), *cert. denied* 282 U.S. 902 (1931).

31. Warner Bros. Pictures, Inc. v. Columbia Broadcasting System, Inc., 216 F.2d 945 (9th Cir. 1954); *see* Borroughs v. Metro-Goldwyn-Mayer, Inc., 683 F.2d 610 (2d Cir. 1982).

32. Williams Electronics, Inc. v. Artic International, Inc., 685 F.2d 870 (3rd Cir. 1982); Apple Computer, Inc. v. Franklin Computer Corp., 714 F.2d 1240 (3rd Cir. 1983), *cert. denied* 464 U.S. 1033 (1984); Apple Computer, Inc. v. Formula International Inc., 562 F.Supp. 775 (N.D. Cal. 1983).

33. Final Report of the National Commission on New Technological Uses of Copyrighted Works, pp. 9–38. Prior law had held that if a work was not intelligible, even with magnification, to the human eye, it neither infringed copyright nor was entitled to copyright. White-Smith Music Publishing Co. v. Apollo Co., 209 U.S. 1 (1908); Corcoran v. Montgomery Ward & Co., Inc., 121 F.2d 572 (9th Cir. 1941). At first it was thought that this doctrine might apply to object code, Data Cash Systems, Inc. v. JS&A Group, Inc., 480 F.Supp. 1063 (N.D.Ill. 1979), *aff'd on other grounds,* 628

F.2d 1038 (7th Cir. 1980). *See* Stern, "Another Look at Copyright Protection of Software: Did the 1980 Act Do Anything for Object Code?" *Computer Law Journal* vol. III, no. 1 (Fall, 1981), pp. 1–17.

34. Final Report of CONTU, at pp. 19–21.

35. Chamberlin v. Uris Sales Corp., 150 F.2d 512 (2d Cir. 1945); *see* Brief English Systems v. Owen, 48F.2d 555 (2d Cir. 1931) and Universal Athletic Sales Co. v. Salkeld, 511 F.2d 904 (3rd Cir. 1975); *cf.* the factually ambiguous case of Runge v. Lee, 441 F.2d 479 (9th Cir. 1971) and Justice Douglas's dissent to the denial of certiorari thereon, 404 U.S. 887 (1971).

36. 797 F.2d 1222 (3d Cir. 1986).

37. Plains Cotton Cooperative Association of Lubbock, Texas v. Goodpasture Computer Service, Inc., 807 F.2d 1256 (5th Cir. 1987).

38. Diamond v. Diehr, 450 U.S. 175 (1981); *see also* Diamond v. Bradley, 600 F.2d 807 (C.C.P.A. 1979), *aff'd by an equally divided court,* 450 U.S. 381 (1981).

39. This and several other patented algorithms are described in a story in the New York Times, February 15, 1989, page D-1. One court has even suggested that patent may be appropriate for a cash management program. Paine, Webber, Jackson & Curtis, Inc. v. Merrill, Lynch, Pierce, Fenner & Smith, Inc., 564 F.Supp. 1358 (D.Del. 1983).

40. 53 Fed. Reg. 21817–21820 (6/10/88); *cf.* Digital Communications Associates, Inc. v. Softklone Distributing Corp., 659 F.Supp. 449 (N.D.Ga. 1987).

41. Manufacturers Technologies, Inc. v. Cams, Inc., 706 F.Supp. 984 (D. Conn. 1989).

42. The Copyright Office has denied registration to at least one screen display on quite traditional grounds. It found the expression in Atari's "Breakout" was so merged with the idea as to be uncopy-

rightable. ("Breakout" is a paddle and ball game, and the display consists of a rectangular paddle directing a ball into colored rectangular bricks with a "pick, pock" sound.) Denial of registration did not by itself, it should be noted, deny the existence of copyright, but in this case the Copyright Office has been upheld on appeal, and a court judgment is indeed conclusive. Atari Games Corp. v. Oman, 8 U.S.P.Q. 2d 1426 (D.D.C. 1988).

43. Manufacturers Technologies, Inc. v. Cams, Inc., *supra.*

44. This reasoning seems to have been overlooked in the recent case of Pearl Systems, Inc. v. Competition Electronics, Inc. 8 U.S.P.Q.2d 1520 (S.D. Fla. 1988). That case, which has already been severely criticized, held a software writer liable for infringement when he had created his own original code to achieve the same results as the plaintiff's program, which was activated by the pushing of buttons.

45. 17 U.S.C. §901 *et seq.*

46. 17 U.S.C. §906(a). Brooktree Corp. v. Advanced Micro Devices, Inc., 705 F.Supp. 491 (S.D.Cal. 1988).

Chapter 2

1. 17 U.S.C. §101.

2. Shapiro, Bernstein & Co. v. Jerry Vogel Music Co., Inc., 161 F.2d 406, 410 (2d Cir. 1946, 1947), *cert. denied* 331 U.S. 820 (1942).

3. H. Rep., p. 120.

4. Sweet Music, Inc. v. Melrose Music Corp., 189 F.Supp. 655, 659 (S.D.Cal. 1960).

5. Melville B. Nimmer, *Nimmer on Copyright* (New York: Matthew Bender, 1980), §6.10[C].

6. *See* Avedon v. Exstein, 141 F.Supp. 278 (S.D.N.Y.

1956); Lumiere v. Pathe Exchange, 275 Fed. 428 (2d Cir. 1921).

7. Brattleboro Publishing Co. v. Winmill Publishing Corp., 369 F.2d 565 (2d Cir. 1966); May v. Morganelli-Heumann & Associates, 618 F.2d 1363, 1368 (9th Cir. 1980).

8. Aldon Accessories Ltd. v. Spiegel, Inc., 738 F.2d 548 (2d Cir. 1984); *accord,* Brunswick Beacon, Inc. v. Schock-Hopchas Publishing Co., 810 F.2d 410 (4th Cir. 1987); Evans Newton, Inc. v. Chicago Systems Software, 793 F.2d 889 (7th Cir. 1986), *cert. denied* 107 S.Ct. 434 (1986).

9. Town of Clarkstown v. Reeder, 566 F.Supp. 137 (S.D.N.Y. 1983).

10. 815 F.2d 323 (5th Cir. 1987).

11. Community for Creative Non-Violence v. Reid, 109 S.Ct. 2166 (1989).

12. Dumas v. Gommerman, 865 F.2d 1093 (9th Cir. 1989).

13. Community for Creative Non-Violence v. Reid, ——— U.S. ——— (1989); Slip Op. No. 88-293 (6/5/89).

14. 20 U.S.C. §109(c).

15. *See* Yojna, Inc. v. American Medical Data Systems, Inc., 667 F.Supp. 446 (E.D.Mich. 1987).

16. Avedon v. Exstein, *supra.*

17. *See* 17 U.S.C. §301(a).

18. 17 U.S.C. §201(b).

19. Van Cleef & Arpels, Inc. v. Schechter, 308 F.Supp. 674 (S.D.N.Y. 1969); Scherr v. Universal Match Corp., 417 F.2d 497 (2d Cir. 1969).

20. 17 U.S.C. §201(b).

21. The Final Report on CONTU only brushes against this problem, at p. 45 *et seq.* Its discussion of the general area seems sketchy.

22. 17 U.S.C. §101.

23. *See* Ringer and Flacks, "Applicability of the Universal Copyright Convention to Certain Works in the Public Domain of Their Country of Origin," *Bull. Copr. Society* vol. 27, no. 3, 1980.

24. *See, e.g.,* Public Affairs Associates, Inc. v. Rickover, 268 F.Supp. 444 (D.D.C. 1967); Bell v. Combined Registry Co., 536 F.2d 164 (7th Cir. 1976).

25. 17 U.S.C. §201(d)(2).

26. 17 U.S.C. §202.

27. 17 U.S.C. §109(b).

28. In re Marriage of Worth, 4 U.S.P.Q. 2d 1730 (Cal.Ct.App. 1987).

29. 17 U.S.C. §904.

30. 17 U.S.C. §302(b).

31. 17 U.S.C. §302(c).

Chapter 3   1. 17 U.S.C. §201(e).

2. Vault Corporation v. Quaid Software, Ltd., 847 F.2d 255 (5th Cir. 1988).

3. David Grossman Designs, Inc. v. Bortin, 347 F.Supp. 1150 (N.D.Ill. 1972); Gerlach-Barklow Co. v. Morris & Bendien, 23 F.2d 159 (2nd Cir. 1927).

4. 17 U.S.C. §204(a).

5. *See, e.g.,* with regard to time limitations, 17 U.S.C.

§203(b)(6); Viacom Int'l, Inc. v. Tandem Productions, Inc., 368 F.Supp. 1264 (S.D.N.Y. 1974), *aff'd* 526 F.2d 593 (2nd Cir. 1975).

6. *See, e.g.*, Bartsch v. Metro-Goldwyn-Mayer, Inc., 391 F.2d 150 (2nd Cir. 1968); Ettore v. Philco Television Broadcasting Corp., 229 F.2d 481 (3rd Cir. 1956). Prof. Nimmer lists many more of these cases at §10.10[B] of Nimmer, *op. cit.*

7. 17 U.S.C. §201(c).

8. Mills Music v. Cromwell Music, 126 F.Supp. 54 (S.D.N.Y. 1954); *cf.* Viacom Int'l, Inc. v. Tandem Productions, Inc., *supra*.

9. 17 U.S.C. §204(a).

10. Nimmer, *op. cit.*, §10.09.

11. 17 U.S.C. §204(a). Eden Toys v. Florelee, 697 F.2d 27 (2d Cir. 1982).

12. 17 U.S.C. §204(b).

13. 17 U.S.C. §405(a)(3).

14. 17 U.S.C. §708(a)(4).

15. 17 U.S.C. §§205(b), 708(a)(9).

16. 17 U.S.C. §205(c).

17. 17 U.S.C. §205(e).

18. *Ibid.*

19. 17 U.S.C. §205(f).

20. 17 U.S.C. §203(a) (5).

21. 17 U.S.C. §§203(a), 203(b) (5).

22. *Ibid.*

23. 17 U.S.C. §203(b)(1); Mills Music, Inc. v. Snyder, 469 U.S. 153 (1985).

24. 17 U.S.C. §§101, 203(a).

25. 17 U.S.C. §203(a)(3).

26. *See generally* 17 U.S.C. §203.

27. 17 U.S.C. §203(b).

28. 17 U.S.C. §203(b)(4).

29. 17 U.S.C. §203(b)(3).

30. *Ibid.*

Chapter 4

1. 17 U.S.C. §401(d), added by P.L. 100–568, 102 Stat. 2853.

2. 17 U.S.C. §101; Jewelers' Mercantile Agency, Ltd. v. Jewelers' Weekly Pub. Co., 155 N.Y. 241, 49 N.E. 872 (1897).

3. Gottsberger v. Aldine Book Pub. Co., 33 Fed. 381 (C.C.D. Mass. 1887); Bobbs-Merrill Co. v. Straus, 147 Fed. 15 (2nd Cir. 1906), *aff'd* 210 U.S. 339 (1908).

4. 17 U.S.C. §101.

5. Grandma Moses Properties, Inc. v. This Week Magazine, 117 F. Supp. 348 (S.D.N.Y. 1953); *cf.* remarks of Rep. Kastenmeier, 122 Cong. Rec. No. 10, 874–5 (daily ed. Sept. 22, 1976).

6. 17 U.S.C. §101.

7. 17 U.S.C. §101; White v. Kimmell, 193 F.2d 744 (9th Cir. 1952).

8. Marvin Worth Prods. v. Superior Films Corp., 319 F. Supp. 1269 (S.D.N.Y. 1970); *see generally* Nimmer, *op. cit.;* §4.10.

9. Folsom v. Marsh, 9 Fed. Cas. 342, No. 4901 (C.C. Mass. 1841).

10. 17 U.S.C. §101.

11. 17 U.S.C. §404(a). This does not apply to ads inserted on behalf of the copyright owner of the collective work.

12. 17 U.S.C. §402.

13. 17 U.S.C. §909(b).

14. 17 U.S.C. §§401(b)(2); 909(b).

15. 17 U.S.C. §§401(b)(3); 408(a).

16. Tonka Corp. v. Tsaisun, Inc., 1 U.S.P.Q.2d 1387 (D. Minn. 1986); *see also* Koontz v. Jaffarian, 787 F.2d 906 (4th Cir. 1986).

17. 17 U.S.C. §406(a).

18. Russell v. Price, 448 F.Supp. 303 (C.D.Cal. 1977).

19. It has been held that omission from 1 percent of 40,000 copies was permissible, whereas omission from 22 to 37 percent of 1,335 copies was not. Original Appalachian Artworks, Inc. v. The Toy Loft, Inc., 684 F.2d 821 (11th Cir. 1982); King v. Burnett, CCH Copr.L.Dec. ¶25,489 (D.D.C. 1982).

20. Compare Shapiro & Son Bedspread Corp. v. Royal Mills Associates, 764 F.2d 69 (2d Cir. 1985), with Forry, Inc. v. Neundorfer, Inc., 837 F.2d 259 (6th Cir. 1988) and cases cited therein.

21. 17 U.S.C. §103(b); Grove Press, Inc. v. Greenleaf Publishing Co., 247 F.Supp. 518 (S.D.N.Y. 1965); Russell v. Price, 612 F.2d 1123 (9th Cir. 1979), *cert. denied* 446 U.S. 952 (1980).

22. 17 U.S.C. §506(c).

23. 17 U.S.C. §406(a).

24. 17 U.S.C. §406(b).

Chapter 5　　1. 17 U.S.C. §411(a).

2. 17 U.S.C. §412. The special exemption for films first fixed at time of broadcast is only available if advance notice is given to an infringer. 17 U.S.C. §411(b), 37 C.F.R. Ch. II §201.22.

3. 17 U.S.C. §910.

4. The Berne Convention Implementation Act ("BCIA"), P.L. 100-568, 102 Stat 2853, declares that lawsuits concerning causes of action arising before March 1, 1989 are governed by the old rules on registration and recordation. BCIA §13 (b). However, this section is captioned "Effect on *pending* cases" (my emphasis). Thus it is unclear whether only cases filed before March 1, 1989 are governed by the old rules, or all cases that could have been filed prior to that date. It appears the latter was intended.

5. The tests described *infra* are embodied in the definitions of the "Berne Convention work" and "country of origin," in 17 U.S.C. §101, as amended by P.L. 100-568, 102 Stat. 2853.

6. The statute is poorly drafted in this respect. Interpreted literally, it would waive registration for any unpublished audiovisual work of which not all authors are legal entities headquartered in the United States; in other words, even if all authors are U.S. citizens, it would waive registration because the authors are not "legal entities." This is clearly not the statutory intent, however.

7. 17 U.S.C. §409.

8. 17 U.S.C. §506(e).

9. 17 U.S.C. §708(a).

10. 17 U.S.C. §407.

11. 37 C.F.R. Ch. II §202.19(f).

12. 17 U.S.C. §407(d).

13. 37 C.F.R. Ch.II §202.19.

14. 37 C.F.R. Ch.II §202.20.

15. 37 C.F.R. Ch.II §202.21.

16. 17 U.S.C. §408(c)(2).

17. 17 U.S.C. §710; 37 C.F.R. Ch. II §201.15.

Chapter 6 1. 17 U.S.C. §117.

2. 17 U.S.C. §109(a).

3. 17 U.S.C. §109(b). Under P.L. 100-617, enacted November 5, 1988, this exception, originally due to expire in 1988, will expire in 1996.

4. 17 U.S.C. §114(a). Congress is considering changing this rule but one can make no predictions.

5. 17 U.S.C. §110.

6. 17 U.S.C. §111(a),(b).

7. 17 U.S.C. §112(b).

8. 37 C.F.R. Ch.II §201.13.

9. 17 U.S.C. §112(d).

10. 17 U.S.C. §110(5).

11. 17 U.S.C. §110(3).

12. 17 U.S.C. §113(c).

13. Gen. Stat. of Conn., Title 42 Sec. 42–116s et seq.; La. Rev. Stat. §51:2151c et seq.; 27 Maine Rev. Stat. §303; Mass. Gen Law Ch. 231 §85S; N.J. Stat. Title 2A, Ch. 24A; N.Y. General Business Law, Art 12-J, §228-

m-q; 73 Penn. Stat. §2101–2110; and Gen. Laws of R.I., Title 5, Ch. 62.

14. Calif. Civil Code §986.

Chapter 7

1. 17 U.S.C. §115. For the royalty rates see 46 Fed. Reg. 55277 (Dec. 23, 1981), and Recording Industry Assoc. v. Copyright Royalty Tribunal, 662 F.2d 1 (D.C. Cir. 1981).

2. 37 C.F.R. Ch.II §201.18.

3. *Ibid.*

4. Sec. 1(e) of the 1909 Act (*i.e.,* of Title 17 as amended prior to enactment of the Copyright Act of 1976); 17 U.S.C. §116(a).

5. Fortnightly Corp. v. United Artists Television, Inc., 392 U.S. 390 (1968).

6. 17 U.S.C. §112. The royalty rates are found at 37 C.F.R. Ch.III Part 308.

7. 17 U.S.C. §501(b),(c),(d).

8. 17 U.S.C. §118.

9. 37 C.F.R. Ch.III Part 304.

Chapter 8

1. A stimulating discussion of this is Prof. Benjamin Kaplan's book, *An Unhurried View of Copyright* (New York: Columbia Univ. Press, 1967).

2. Judge Learned Hand, writing in Nichols v. Universal Pictures Corp., 45 F.2d 119 (2nd Cir. 1930), *cert. denied,* 282 U.S. 902 (1931).

3. *See, e.g.,* Harold Lloyd Corp. v. Witwer, 65 F.2d 1 (9th Cir. 1933); Twentieth Century Fox-Film Corp. v. Stonesifer, 140 F.2d 579 (9th Cir. 1944).

4. Sheldon v. Metro-Goldwyn Pictures Corp., 81 F.2d 49 (2nd Cir., 1936).

5. Bleistein v. Donaldson Lithographing Co., 188 U.S. 239 (1903).

6. Burrow-Giles Lithographic Co. v. Sarony, 111 U.S. 53 (1884).

7. 17 U.S.C. §301(b)(2).

8. 17 U.S.C. §501(b).

9. *Ibid.*

10. 17 U.S.C. §504(b).

11. 17 U.S.C. §504(c).

12. 17 U.S.C. §505.

13. 17 U.S.C. §506(a).

14. 17 U.S.C. §107. On the first criterion, see Rubin v. Boston Magazine Co., 645 F.2d 80 (1st Cir. 1981). On the fourth, see New Boston Television, Inc. v. Entertainment Sports Programming Network, Inc., 215 U.S.P.Q. 755 (D. Mass. 1981); DC Comics, Inc. v. Reel Fantasy, Inc., 696 F.2d 24 (2d Cir. 1982).

15. Publications Int'l Ltd. v. Bally Mfg. Corp., 215 U.S.P.Q. 861 (N.D.Ill. 1982).

16. *See* Meredith Corp. v. Harper & Row, Publishers, Inc., 378 F. Supp. 686 (S.D.N.Y. 1977), *aff'd.* 500 F.2d 1221 (2nd Cir. 1974).

17. 17 U.S.C. §113(c); Italian Book Corp. v. American Broadcasting Companies, Inc., 458 F.Supp. 65 (S.D.N.Y. 1978).

18. Harper & Row, Publishers, Inc. v. The Nation Enterprises, 471 U.S. 539, 105 S. Ct. 2218 (1985).

19. Salinger v. Random House, Inc., 811 F.2d 90 (2d Cir. 1987), *cert. denied*, 108 S. Ct. 213 (1987); New ERA Publications International, ApS v. Henry Holt & Co.,

10 U.S.P.Q. 2d 1561 (2d Cir. 1989), *rev'g* 695 F.Supp. 1493 (S.D.N.Y. 1988).

20. Berne Convention, Paris Text, Art. 10.

21. 131 F. Supp. 165 (S.D. Cal. 1955), *aff'd. sub nom.* Benny v. Loew's, Inc., 239 F.2d 532 (9th Cir. 1956).

22. Columbia Pictures Corp. v. National Broadcasting Co., 137 F. Supp. 348, 350 (S.D.Cal. 1955).

23. *Ibid.*

24. Robert Stigwood Group, Ltd. v. O'Reilly, 346 F.Supp. 376 (D.Conn. 1972).

25. Time, Inc. v. Bernard Geis Associates, 293 F.Supp. 130 (S.D.N.Y. 1968).

26. Scherr v. Universal Match Corp., 297 F. Supp. 102 (S.D.N.Y. 1967).

27. Sony Corporation of America v. Universal City Studios, Inc., 464 U.S. 417 (1984).

28. H. Rep., p. 74.

29. *Ibid.*, p. 73.

30. Basic Books, Inc. v. Gnomon Corp., D. Conn. 1980, Civ. Action No. 80-36.

31. H. Rep., pp. 73–74.

32. *Ibid.*, pp. 68–70.

33. *Ibid.*, pp. 70–71. The text as reprinted here, however, reflects a change in A.2 that was made after the House Report was printed. See remarks of Rep. Kastenmeier in the House Congressional Record for September 22, 1976, at p. 31980.

34. H.R. Conf. Rep. No. 94-1733, 2nd Sess. 70, 1976 U.S. Code Cong. & Ad. News 5659, 5811.

35. 17 U.S.C. §108.

36. 17 U.S.C. §108(d).

37. Final Report of CONTU, pp. 54–55.

38. H. Rep., p. 77.

39. 17 U.S.C. §108(f)(1).

40. Lane v. First National Bank of Boston, 10 U.S.P.Q. 2d 1268 (1st Cir. 1989).

Chapter 9

1. Heim v. Universal Pictures Co., Inc., 154 F.2d 480 (2nd Cir. 1946).

2. Former Title 17 of the U.S. code, §§19, 21.

3. L & L White Metal Casting Corp. v. Cornell Metal Specialties Corp., 353 F. Supp. 1170 (E.D.N.Y. 1972), *aff'd.* 177 U.S.P.Q. 673 (2nd Cir. 1973); First American Artificial Flowers, Inc. v. Joseph Markovits, Inc., 342 F. Supp. 178 (S.D.N.Y. 1972).

4. Copyright Act of 1976, P. L. 94–53, §§103, 108.

5. Goodis v. United Artists Television, Inc., 425 F.2d 397 (2nd Cir. 1970).

6. Group Publishers v. Winchell, 86 F. Supp. 573, 576 (S.D.N.Y. 1952). However, this recordation requirement might well apply still to other types of works; see former Title 17 of the U.S. Code, §32.

7. Pushman v. New York Graphic Society, Inc., 287 N.Y. 302, 39 N.E.2d 249 (1942); Chamberlain v. Feldman, 300 N.Y. 135, 89 N.E.2d 863 (1949).

8. N.Y. Laws 1966, Ch. 688, §3; California Civ. Code, §982(e).

9. Picture Music, Inc. v. Bourne, Inc., 457 F.2d 1213 (2nd Cir. 1972). *Cf.*, Shapiro, Bernstein & Co. v. Jerry

Vogel Music Co., 221 F.2d 569 (2nd Cir. 1955), *mod. on other grounds on rehearing* 223 F.2d 252 (2nd Cir. 1955).

10. Shapiro, Bernstein & Co., Inc. v. Jerry Vogel Music Co., Inc., *supra;* Donna v. Dodd, Mead & Co., Inc., 374 F. Supp. 429 (S.D.N.Y. 1974).

11. White-Smith Pub. Co. v. Apollo Co., *supra.*

12. *See, generally,* Nimmer, *op. cit.,* §2.10.

13. 17 U.S.C. §301(c).

14. Rosette v. Rainbo Record Mfg. Corp., 354 F. Supp. 1183 (S.D.N.Y. 1973), *aff'd* 546 F.2d 461 (2nd Cir. 1976). *See, generally,* Nimmer, *op. cit.,* §4.05.

15. Epoch Producing Corp. v. Killiam Shows, Inc., 522 F.2d 737 (2nd Cir. 1975).

16. Miller Music Company v. Chas. N. Daniels, Inc., 362 U.S. 373 (1960).

17. Fred Fisher Music Co. v. M. Witmark & Sons, 318 U.S. 643 (1943).

18. Marks Music Corp. v. Borst Music Pub. Co., 110 F.Supp. 923 (D.N.J. 1953). For an excellent discussion of these rules and their many quirks, see Nevins, "The Magic Kingdom of Will-Bumping: Where Estates Law and Copyright Law Collide," *Jrnl. Copr. Soc.* vol. 35, no. 2, January 1988.

19. De Sylva v. Ballentine, 351 U.S. 570 (1956); 17 U.S.C. §304(a), 101.

20. Rose v. Bourne, Inc., 279 F.2d 79 (2d Cir. 1960).

21. Edward B. Marks Music Corp. v. Jerry Vogel Music Company, 140 F.2d 266 (2nd Cir. 1944); *but see* Nimmer, *op. cit.,* §9.05[E].

22. Bartok v. Boosey & Hawkes, Inc., 523 F.2d 941 (2d Cir. 1975).

23. H. Rep., p. 139.

24. Former Title 17 of the U.S. Code, §24; *see* Shapiro, Bernstein & Co. v. Bryan, 123 F.2d 1697 (2d Cir. 1941).

25. Abend v. MCA, Inc., 863 F.2d 1465 (9th Cir. 1988); *compare* Rohauer v. Killiam Shows, Inc., 551 F.2d 484 (2d Cir. 1977), *cert. denied* 431 U.S. 949 (1977).

26. 17 U.S.C. §304(a).

27. 17 U.S.C. §408(c)(3).

28. 17 U.S.C. §304.

29. 17 U.S.C. §304(c).

30. *Ibid.;* 37 C.F.R. Ch.II, §201.10.

Chapter 10   1. Rev. Rul. 68-194, 1968-1 C.B. 87.

2. C. W. Churchman, 68 T.C. 696 (1977).

3. I.R.S. Pub. 334, Reg. §1.183-2.

4. Rev. Rul. 73-395, 1972-2 C.B. 87, as affected by P.L. 94-455, §2119. *See* Stern v. U.S.A., 1971-1 U.S.T.C. ¶86,491 (C.D.Cal. 1971).

5. Reg. §1.167(a)-1(b).

6. Rev. Rul. 60-358, 1960-2 C.B. 68.

7. *Ibid.*

8. Rev. Rul. 68-194, 1968-1 C.B. 87.

9. Reg. §1.167(a)-6(a); Rev. Rul. 73-395, 1973-2 C.B. 87, as affected by P.L. 94-455, §2119.

10. Heim v. Fitzpatrick, 262 F.2d 887 (2d Cir. 1959).

11. Rev. Rul. 55-706, 1955-2 C.B. 300.

12. This is by analogy to patents. See Reg. §1.1235-2(b)(2)(ii).

13. Cory v. Commissioner of Internal Revenue, 230 F.2d 941 (2d Cir. 1956), *cert. den.* 35 U.S. 828 (1956); for a patent analogy *see* Marco (1955), 25 T.C. 544.

Chapter 11

1. For a compendium of U.S. copyright relations with foreign countries, see Copyright Office Circular 38a.

2. Berne Convention (Paris Text), Article 7(8). For a detailed discussion of this, particularly as it affects works of the U.S. Government, *see* Ringer and Flacks, *op. cit.*, at pp. 157–204.

3. Berne (Paris Text), Appendix; U.C.C. Arts. Vter, V quarter.

4. Nimmer, *op. cit.*, §17.07[B].

Index